Pages from a Diary

Pages from a Diary
in the life of faith

by

Kenneth S. Roundhill

HODDER AND STOUGHTON
LONDON SYDNEY AUCKLAND TORONTO

Contents

A Biographical Note

KENNETH ROUNDHILL is a New Zealander, his parents
having emigrated from Yorkshire. He is a graduate of Otago
University, Dunedin, graduating in History and Philosophy,
and also from the Bible College of New Zealand.

While engaged as a travelling secretary for the Inter-
Varsity Fellowship in New Zealand he heard God's call to
work among students in Japan and left New Zealand in
1950, having joined the Worldwide Evangelisation Crusade.
He arrived in Japan in early 1951 and was invited to join the
teaching staff of a Theological Academy in Tokyo where for
two years he taught a course introducing the New Testament
through interpretation. Most of the students were graduates
who had been won to Christ through the personal work of
fellow students on campus in the early days of the Kirisu-
tosha Gakusei Kai — or what was then called the I.V.C.F. in
Japan. This work had begun in 1947 through the conversion
of a key student in Waseda University. Teaching on the staff
of this Academy brought Ken into a close fellowship with
some who were destined to be the first national staff workers
of the movement. He himself began to visit the campuses to
lead Bible study groups and later was officially asked to
become a staff worker for the movement, a relationship that
continues to this day.

After the appointing of national staff in the Tokyo area,
Ken felt that it was time he moved into another strategic

student area and left for Kobe after about four years in Tokyo. After a year or so in Kobe he married a Canadian who had been on the staff of the Teachers' Christian Fellowship there. They shifted to Kyoto, a city of over 1,300,000 people and over forty University and Junior Colleges. Very soon Ken was asked to assume the leadership responsibilities for the Mission which worked in the province near Kyoto. This, alongside his K.G.K. staff work, involved not only overall administration for an international team of some twenty-six missionaries, but pastoral work at the weekends in Mission-related churches.

This Mission leadership responsibility continued for some fourteen years till the time came when he thought the Japanese Pastors, who were converts of the work, should form a constitution for the national church that had come into being through the work of the missionaries. As a result, the nationals asked that the Mission should be integrated into the church and that the fellowship that had grown between nationals and foreigners should continue. Ken resigned from leadership and for a period acted as assistant to the Japanese Chairman who was much his junior, and who now became the overall leader for church and Mission. When due to go on furlough he resigned his remaining posts as a leader and committee member, and the two key leadership posts were taken by Japanese, with an overall governing body of four nationals and two foreigners.

Although free from Mission duties, Ken now has oversight and some preaching responsibilities for a church in Kyoto and continues to help in the spread of Bible study groups in the Colleges and in the training of student leaders and conference work. At the same time, there has been a sense of call to help in the training of Japanese for missionary work abroad. To this end, he now edits a monthly prayer calendar of news items for students and his home is used for an orientation course for Japanese preparing to go abroad, specially after they have graduated from Bible School or Seminary. Recently one young lady who had lived with them for some time for this purpose left for a prolonged visit to Malaysia, trusting that in some way the door will open for her to serve the Lord there.

The missionary vision is growing among the students of Japan and this calls for regular training meetings and special addresses at the seasonal conferences. So far, only a very small beginning has been made, but Ken and Betty feel that this could be perhaps a major contribution for them in their remaining days of service in Japan.

Preface

THERE ARE SO MANY facets of the life of faith it is worth living longer just to experience some more! That my thirty-nine years as a Christian have not exhausted all the possibilities will certainly be obvious enough — not that all are experienced with equal delight, as I hope I have been honest enough to indicate.

I happen to be a missionary. This to some, immediately places me in a category apart. Missionaries, in a special sense, are supposed to live by faith. This, of course, is nonsense. I know many of God's children in their home countries who are living by faith in the most realistic, adventurous and demanding way. The life of faith does not have to do just with paying exorbitant rents in a culture determined to exploit the supposedly affluent foreigner, with meeting sky-rocketing language tuition fees, and paying the milkman three times the price for what you hope is the equivalent of what you drink so nonchalantly at home.

That this selection of diary entries does have its experiences of financial deliverances and testing will not invalidate this either. What I hope the enclosed record will show is that the faith of the Lord's children anywhere includes trusting Him when He seems to contradict Himself. There is also the patience of faith, for often we just have to wait for the fullness of God's time, for He knows best when to fulfil His Own promises for our good. There is the rest of faith, that takes the strain out of the kind of life that equates busyness with usefulness. I've had my ulcer too!

There is also the obedience of faith that means we find ourselves obeying impossible commands, and taking steps that run contrary to commonsense just because we know the Lord will interpret the significance of His plans with each successive step. We have learnt to trust Him with the after-wards of obedience. These and other aspects of the life of faith may have little or nothing to do with money as you will see.

On the other hand, some misapplied Old Testament promises and the enormous pressure of materialistic opinion upon us today have conditioned many into thinking that a well-lined pocket is a synonym for God's blessing. Any kind of life that is not well padded with earthly prom-ises, legitimate 'rights', and built-in age benefits is not glori-fying to God. I hope the testimony of these pages will do something to show up this fallacy and add one more voice to the many who have insisted that you take no real risk when you step out on the promises of the Lord alone.

Marriage has to be included in this, because life then becomes both a corporate act of faith, and a daily experi-ence of faith together. It is one of the enormous privileges of the Christian life that the Lord takes such a big hand in finding one's life partner. Then, as a team of faith it has been precious to have the Lord speaking to us separately and simultaneously with the assurances we have needed in times of crisis. He has burdened us independently to pray for the same things, and in one case, only when the answer came did we delightedly find we had been under similar constraint.

In some mysterious way it would appear that He needs us to pray for the thing that He intends to do, and He moves us to pray accordingly. Someone has said that God does nothing but in answer to prayer. In whatever measure that is true, it leaves you with an awe-ful feeling that if we lived a whole lot closer to the Lord, we would no doubt be trusted with more of His soliloquies and be available for more frequent briefings and prayerful assignments.

The incidents recorded here are all factual. Naturally I cannot remember the actual date of the earlier entries and did not keep a diary till after I reached the Mission field in 1951, but the circumstances of what is recorded are as clear to me as if I were reading them from an extant diary. For this reason I have taken the liberty of guessing some early dates, and presenting the material in the format you see, in the hope that it will add interest to the reading. This is but a book of human testimony. My prayer is that its reading will stimulate a more experimental confidence in the Lord Himself, and in His Word that He delights to honour.

     K.S.R.

     Kyoto, Japan

1

Faith's Irreducible Minimum

6 June 1924

'Saw the wild horse today. The kids sed it wud eat me.
I had to drive the cows past. I praid so the other kids did
not see me. It went away quick.'

THE DATE IS A wild guess and an eight-year-old is far too busy living to keep a diary, even if he could write one. So the wording and spelling are, of course, a Milne-like attempt to get back into my Christopher Robin shoes — if I wore any, which I doubt. The facts remain with me with crystal clarity. It was my duty each afternoon to drive my father's cows to a paddock at the end of our road for pasture. On the way home from school, children in the neighbourhood had assured me that a wild horse was in one of the paddocks I had to pass. Sure enough, as I approached, a snorting monster of a stallion had its head over the hedge glaring at me. I was terrified. The cows sauntered on but I was rooted to the spot.

I leaned over a post on the side of the road, as if examining some insects, for I could not bear to let local pals see me pray. Closing my eyes, as I thought necessary to be decent or heard, I shot up an agonised plea to heaven for deliverance. When I looked up the horse had already wheeled and was about to gallop to the other end of the paddock. I cannot remember now if I took the trouble to voice any thanks but my profound sense of relief still lingers with me. Whether experiences like this encouraged me to toddle off alone to Sunday School, I do not know. The nightly prayer with Mother beside me was a perfunctory gesture but the habit thus inculcated was beneficial even if the words were rote-like and merely from the lips. It was to be another ten years before I again prayed with any real agony of desire. This time it was for deliverance from the felt presence of the devil and for an assurance of salvation. The reply was just as ready and explicit.

I have reached into the past for this incident because I find it touches on a grown-up problem. You see, in both of these instances I had prayed the 'prayer of faith'. In the first case, I had a very vague idea of a God of the Universe. It never occurred to me to doubt Him. But I was quite clueless about the coming of the Lord Jesus. I was not consciously praying to God the Father through the merit and sacrifice of His Son. If we can only come to God knowing that we come through the Lord Jesus, then I was trespassing. Or was I?

An easy way out of this dilemma would be to write off my prayer as just an instinctive cry for help to any higher power around. I have known blaspheming pagans to do this in slit trenches when the enemy bombs were falling. They forgot their prayers very quickly when the dust settled. If I had been brought up a Japanese Buddhist, I might have turned instinctively to Shaka Sama. To some, it would have been quite a coincidence that the horse turned just at that psychological time.

A more sophisticated and theological answer might be that I was obviously the child of at least a believing mother and as such was 'holy', as Paul states in I Corinthians 7:14. Actually, Paul does not go on to spell out what he meant by that, though Christians who believe that God has a covenant with believing parents and their children whom they offer to Him in a dedication, christening or baptismal service while still babes in arms, would be happy to think that I was being heard for my mother's sake and because of her faith in the Saviour.

Perhaps so, but this does not answer all my queries. I have seen young people with no Christian parentage who gave tangible evidence of being born again, but for the life of them they could not understand or explain what had happened in biblical terms. Here in Japan, it is not uncommon for someone to profess faith in Christ and after attending meetings for some time and taking an intelligent part in prayer, suddenly, to the consternation of the missionary, ask just who Jesus Christ was anyway. A similar question will be asked about the meaning of the cross. While still without a clear understanding of what we feel to be absolutely basic to a saving faith, some evidences of real life in Christ may be seen. In my own life, I confess that I had little or no conviction of sin when I reached out in desperation to God in prayer for salvation, as I will describe in a later chapter. The conviction of what sin really is and its loathsomeness in me only came subsequently to a saving experience. This also is not consistent with all those neat rules one is supposed to follow these days to find God.

My question is therefore, just how much faith do we need? What is faith's irreducible minimum? What doctrinal content to real faith is needed if we are going to get through to God, for as the Bible says quite explicitly, 'Without faith it is impossible to please Him, for he that cometh to God must believe that He is and that He is the rewarder of them that diligently seek Him' (Hebrews 11:6).

A pastor friend here in Japan was called the 'beer barrel' when a young man because of his drinking habits. Largely because of his dissolute habits he was sick. Leaving the hospital one day he strolled into a tent meeting and heard a message that transformed his life. What was the substance of that message? Simply, and this was the first time he had ever heard of such a thing, that there was but one God and He was a living God. His response was that if there was indeed one living God then he was determined to serve Him. His drinking habits left him. He returned home to get rid of all the idols in his house. His wife was so astonished at the change in her husband she began to go to church. Today he is a greatly loved pastor of a country church. Naturally, further instruction soon followed on that simple but powerful grasp of some elementary truths but these profound changes in his life did not wait until he had been soundly instructed in the fundamentals of the faith. It would seem that it is not the amount one knows but the degree of capitulation to the little truth one hears that counts.

I believe there is a close connection between this problem and the fact that the Lord seems, on occasion, to reach down sovereignly to touch individuals perhaps in the remote tribal fastness or the most sophisticated life in some concrete jungle and stir hearts to seek Him. The interesting thing that invariably comes out of the record of their ultimate conversion is, that though they receive some vision or add another altar 'to the unknown God' to the others already in the house, all this is but preparation for the coming of the missionary or the hearing of the Gospel in some form or other before real saving faith is experienced.

I know of a native in primitive jungle life who suddenly had a vision of a white man coming to him with a book. This vision prepared his heart for the reception of the message when the missionary did in fact visit the tribe. Not only the man, but the whole tribe, was found to be friendly and disposed to listen without prejudice. A lass in the country here in Japan had, from childhood, a profound love of beauty in any form. The stars at night were her constant delight. Although her home was full of 'gods many' she felt that there must be a God big enough and wonderful enough for the vastness and the beauty of things in the universe. It was no surprise therefore that she responded to the Gospel the first night she heard and has remained a consistent Christian ever since. The Lord Jesus was obviously the answer to all that she had ever longed for. The Lord had both put the longing there and then sent the missionary to give faith's saving Object. Even the Ethiopian eunuch, notwithstanding that the very Book was on his knees and he read it with reverence, needed the ministry of Philip the evangelist to point out the way in which Christ fulfilled all the promises of a coming Saviour and Messiah.

Now all this leads me to believe that the Lord is sensitive

to the merest breathings of longing for Himself. Even if our faith reaches but the hem of His garment — superstitious and so very immature — yet, He is quick to see that His saving power is not squandered by ignorance and hastens to instruct us as to faith's Object. It encourages me to be patient with some who don't have the right formulae and pat phrases. It cautions me not to force open the bud when the season for the full bloom of faith has not yet arrived.

2

Faith's Committal

16 March 1934

'The Lord used a Marxist to bring me to Himself today! After the usual mental battering much of the day at work, I wondered tonight if there was any point to reading the Bible again. But the thought of a God-less existence and death like a dog was appalling. I knelt to read as usual and the passage tonight happened to be John, chapter 10. Verse 28 reads: '. . . and I give unto them eternal life, and they shall never perish, and no one shall snatch them out of my hand.' There came the strangest sense that Satan was trying to snatch me out of God's hand. Intellectually, my fellow worker had almost convinced me that God did not exist and the Bible was a man-made superstitious fabrication. In utter confusion, I cried out: 'Oh God, if there be a God, save me now!' Then, right then, what amazing peace He gave. Oh, the indescribable sense of belonging, of being utterly safe in Him, of being possessed and yet free for the first time.'

NEXT DAY, THE PRESSURE was still on. The Marxist had found out that I was a church-goer so he left his anti-government, anti-boss invective that had filled every lunch hour and turned on me again. The interesting thing was that this time, though intellectually I was no better prepared to meet his anti-God invective than I had been the day before, his arguments did not trouble me in the least! The day before they had been devastating. I can still remember walking home at night deeply distressed at the thought of being, as he insisted, a spirit-less being with no after life and just the victim of blind chance and materialistic forces.

The reason why a Marxist should be an unwitting instrument in my spiritual experience makes sense now that I look back. Because of a Godly mother's life and influence and some Sunday School attendance, I had never had any occasion to doubt the existence of God. When very lonely, I was befriended by an outstanding group of young Christian men and happily joined their Bible class. Later, I went through the motions of a profession of personal faith. It was the 'done thing'. I knew how to pray the appropriate words when being counselled and I fully expected to be overcome with joy afterwards, as had been the experience of a famous Christian the pastor was fond of speaking about. Apparently, on his way home, he felt that the very snowflakes were singing their praises with him to his new found Saviour. For me, there were neither snowflakes nor singing. I wanted the joy but God had His own gentle way of getting me to the place of reality and to the end of my self-righteous ways and pride before He could give that in full measure.

Mine was a second-hand faith. I parroted the things that were being said by those I loved and admired. I was drifting along in a pleasant world of Christian make-believe just for the sheer pleasure of being wanted by good people and, I rather hoped, appreciated. Only one of them seemed to see through the sham and he had the courage on one occasion to ask if I was really a Christian. I replied with rather an indignant 'yes', for I can still remember my feelings being ruffled. But I could not shake off the troubled feeling his question evoked. I could not doubt the reality of *his* Christian experience and so if he did not think I was a Christian, what was missing? I didn't know. I was just too proud to ask him personally and so went about things in a more formal way and ended up as puzzled as ever.

Shock treatment was God's answer. I needed shaking out of a mere acquiescence to the truth so that faith in Christ stood over against the only other logical alternative — materialism. Not that I could reason with my unhappy critic. It was years before I could have stood up to him on an intellectual level and argued point by point on the inadequacy of materialism from a scientific point of view. At that time, I needed to see that faith that touched God was something beyond reason — above it — and later, with the privileges of academic study, there would come the conviction that faith was not opposed to reason. As Francis Schaeffer has suggested. I had to give up my rationalism and hold on to my rationality.

In the earlier quest for reality, I had equated being a Christian with feelings of joy, faith with ecstasy, and was disappointed. In seeking first the joy, I was missing the very faith that brings it. Joy, in company with most of the other pleasant emotions of Christian experience, is a by-product of something else. We don't get it by seeking it for itself.

Surely one of the purest joys comes when we inadvertently discover that we have been used to bring real joy to someone else.

The brush with militant materialism was strong medicine for a common malaise in church circles. I was faced with an ultimatum and could no longer drift. To change the figure, I had been supported upright just by the weight of public opinion, like a commuter in a crowded Japanese tram in the rush hour. There is no need to strap hang! But suddenly the crowd disappears. There is no one to lean on. There is no strap to grab. Fortunately, Someone grabbed me. Or, it would be truer to say, in the famous confession: 'I hold and am held.' Both are true in that reaching out to God in faith.

The very circumstances of my conversion and the tension that precipitated a total commitment through intellectual confrontation, had its effect in stimulating a keen interest in apologetics. The world soon became a place of infinite wonder and fascination to me. People suddenly changed, I thought. They were more precious — each one differently so. Of course, it was I who had changed. I seemed to wake up intellectually as well as spiritually. I had become somewhat like a first-class passenger on a liner that still had the first- and second-class passenger decks. On such lines, second-or third-class passengers are not permitted to trespass on the upper decks. I had become a kind of first-class passenger in God's universe, for not only could I feel at home in the realm of the Spirit but I could roam all over the 'other decks', so to speak. I could now revel in God's handiwork in nature and His purposes in history and study these with all the help that science could provide and my capacity for study could assimilate. The non-Christian, no matter how well-schooled a scientist, is confined to his second-class 'deck' and the realm of the Spirit is closed to him.

This privilege in the Christian life has been well illustrated in the life of Duncan M. Blair, Regium Professor of Anatomy in the University of Glasgow, 1936–44. Dr. M.

Lloyd-Jones has pointed out that, 'here was an anatomist, of all things an expert in a subject that can be so dry and mechanical, moreover, an anatomist profoundly interested in the subjects of morphology, comparative anatomy, and genetics, and yet one who was not merely Christian in the formal general sense, but actively and militantly. The subjects which are supposed to account for the scepticism and unbelief of so many went to confirm and increase his faith. He thereby demonstrated (what the Bible teaches everywhere) that unbelief has its origin in the heart and not in the mind.'

According to Duncan Blair, 'The Bible is not contrary to science. In thirty years of biological study I have learned nothing that in the slightest degree diminishes my faith in God or my belief in the Bible as His uniquely inspired Word ... On the contrary, my scientific studies have helped to deepen my faith and on occasion to enrich my understanding of God's Word.'

I am tremendously grateful that the encounter with militant anti-supernaturalism took place before university studies became possible. Having been captured for Christ and with a mind now both subject to His daily influence through the Word and eager to know more of Himself through His handiwork, further academic opposition to my faith only served as a stimulus to find the kind of truth that is never the enemy of truth. Admittedly, then as now, there were insoluble problems. Both in science and Scripture, I came across the apparent contradiction that just had to be laid aside till further light was forthcoming. In the realm of the Spirit there are also questions in my heart to which I doubt I will find an answer till I see the Lord, face to face. Then, as Paul says, 'we shall know as we are known.' At the same time, I must confess that I know enough, more than enough, to make me a convinced Christian. In other words, there are so many indubitable evidences of God at work in His universe that I would have to commit intellectual suicide to try to avoid the God I have come to know. No matter how poorly I represent Him, He fills my horizon with more light than I can contain. Faith therefore, to me, is the most reasonable thing in the world — faith in Him, that is.

3

Faith's 'Culture Shock'

20 July 1935

'Tonight, the bottom dropped out of my world. I owe so much to him as a spiritual leader. I know that he is a praying man, a man of God. I know that he is a true scholar of the Bible and loves it. How could he possibly get angry, and that with his own son, and before us all? He could have slapped me personally in the face, the shock was so great. Frankly, I think his son was in the right too. Lord, how can I listen to his preaching now with any respect and confidence? Where can I find consistency and perfection?'

IN THE EARLY DAYS of my Christian life, faith in God and faith in God's men were bound up into one bundle of inter-dependent experience. I was still young enough to be some-what of a hero worshipper. The love of God had flooded my heart and brought me into a fellowship and relationship with His children that was exceedingly precious to me. I think I knew real love, or felt real love, for the first time, for in my own family, one's feelings were rigorously suppressed. If we loved each other, we showed it in any other way than a demonstration of affection. The felt love of Christ brought a new release and with it the capacity to love my family and then, in a very special sense, to love those who had now become my brothers and sisters in Christ. Now that love was wounded, grieved. Ultimately, the whole experience threw me back upon Christ in a new way but at the time, it seemed to make Him a more distant Person — a God away out there — infinitely great in contrast to people who so poorly represented Him. This contrast seemed to make Him the more unapproachable. I was bewildered.

When idealism had been tempered with objectivity, Bible knowledge, and an increasing distress at my own failures, my fallen idol became a fellow sinner for whom I knew I had to pray. No more could I treat him like an animated Bible or a rare exhibit in God's glass case, reserved for special weekend exhibitions.

At that time I had little or no appreciation of the difference one's temperament makes to one's reactions in a time of moral or emotional crisis. I was, and still am, phlegmatic. Anger appalled me. He was probably a choleric and though this was the only occasion on which I saw him show anger, I do know that he had the capacity for the kind of righteous indignation and decided protest action that put him in the vanguard of a vigorous evangelical thrust that left its wholesome mark on the city for years. Others might feel deeply, but are neither coherent enough to be forceful in debate nor timely in their protests. My trouble as a phlegmatic, is that crucial issues leave me profoundly disturbed but I am too slow in my reactions for instant and timely interjection. To be honest, there are times when I have nothing to say anyway. Being forced to say something would only reveal the embarrassing fact that the vacant look indicates the vacant mind. At least in silence some will give you the benefit of the doubt and imagine that you have a lot to say but are wisely restrained.

If I do feel very deeply about something but have had no time to sort out my reasons, I tend to become more incoherent as more moral and vocal pressure is put upon me. This is why it is so much easier for me to write my judgments down when the dust has settled. However, it would hardly do for all leaders in Christian confrontation and controversy to have to retire to their respective closets to prepare their carefully thought out replies in any verbal exchange. Phlegmatics have their place, but it is certainly not in the quick exchange of public debate. I mention this because while the choleric has to ask the Lord's help in restraining a turbulent spirit and the hasty word, it behoves the phlegmatic to restrain his judgment when he finds himself critical of the choleric Christian leader.

Then, with a growing knowledge of the Bible and its faithful treatment of the weaknesses and failures of its leading personalities, I came to realise that they were not used in proportion to their perfection. I recall my instant (on this occasion, at least) and horrified reaction at my father's remark that King David had committed both adultery and murder. Father at this time, was embittered and critical of Christian things. He used David's sin as an excuse for his own distrust of the Bible in particular and Christianity as a whole. He had been sorely grieved by the conduct of a professing Christian in business. Unfortunately, he had not read carefully enough to recall the fact that though David was personally forgiven his sin upon his repentance, the continuing effect of that sin as it worked out in the lives of his family and later the whole nation was horrendous. My reaction to father's criticism stemmed from the fact that I knew David to be the author of all those wonderful Psalms in the Bible. How could he possibly have written them if he had committed the 'worst' of sins; the two worst in current thinking? In fact, I doubted if David could be in the Bible at all in those circumstances. Perhaps father had confused him with another David.

Both father and I were wrong. We both needed to know that David also wrote Psalm 51, the penitential Psalm wherein he confessed his sin and sought forgiveness and restoration. Has any Psalm, next perhaps to that of Psalm 23, the Psalm of the Shepherd, been used to bring such comfort and blessing as this heartfelt cry for forgiveness? God uses people who have sinned greatly, but only if they have repented and shown the fruit of that repentance in a hatred of the sin that caused the Lord's grief. Like Peter, they love the Lord all the more for the wonder of His forgiveness.

Think of the quarrel between Paul and Barnabas. Feelings must have run quite high between them (Acts 15:36-40) when they quarrelled over the matter of including Mark with them in their evangelistic journeys. Verse 31 says, 'And there arose a sharp contention so that they separated from each other.' Paul obviously was of a choleric disposition and reacted quite firmly in his likes and dislikes and quite openly in all his opinions. Time was to prove him wrong. Mark became very useful to Paul himself and also to the whole church for all time. It could well be that the crisis over his suitability at that time and the grief over the separation of the two great friends may have had a salutary effect upon the young man Mark and contributed to his needed discipline. If that were the case, then both Paul and Barnabas were right. Their parting, though painful to them both at the time, contributed not only to Mark's growth in character but it also served to ensure that two teams were established and that the experiences of these two veterans were shared with younger men who joined them afterwards.

After being on the mission field for some years, I have come to see that differences between Christian workers, missionaries or leaders are not necessarily calamitous. Some of us, disposition-wise, are incompatible. One type will only baffle and irk another type — even though both are of equal zeal. We can and should love each other fervently and respect each other's opinions and methods. But we are not meant to mimic each other nor all work together. Some of us need the cross currents of a differing opinion to get our own thinking on a more scriptural basis. The more choleric may 'lose his cool' for quite a number of reasons and still find a place of ready repentance towards God and reconciliation with his grieved brother Christian. Indeed a mark of the choleric seems to be the unpremeditated and unrestrained outburst of frustration but with an equal readiness to forgive, to forget and bear no grudges upon reconciliation. All this I was not to know when faith had its first 'culture shock'!

Personal failure also later injected some much needed humility into the criticism of other Christians. If I didn't lose my cool in public, I might sin more grievously in private. Worse still, as a Christian I could repeat the same sin, vowing always of course to do better next time or not to repeat the same thing. I am convinced now that the reason why we fail in the same way again is because we do not despair of ourselves profoundly enough. We think that we will know better next time. Sometimes, we vainly hope for some ecstatic experience that will deliver us from being that kind of a person. Even victory in this realm cannot be taken for granted, for we can fail again. Faith, therefore, has come to mean to me, a moment by moment looking to and utter dependence upon the Lord Jesus. Even if there is no overt sin, the sense of inward failure and worthlessness can be so keen that unless I look to Jesus for my complete fulfilment and know that God joys in me for His Son's sake, I can lose heart and give way to the kind of despair that carries with it no healing, but in fact a departure from the Lord Himself.

4

Faith's Practice

19 April 1939

'Here I am in Bible college but how am I going to pay my fees? I was sure I could sell my car. If Bob hadn't promised to buy it and then changed his mind after the peak selling time, I could have sold it to someone else. I was relying on that sale for most of this year's fees. In fact, the promised sale of that car I took to be a seal on my coming into Bible college. And now what? What's the Lord trying to say to me? To be honest, I've got some misgivings about having bought that car in the first place. I can see now that my motives were pretty mixed. I've got a lot to learn about stewardship. But what am I going to do? I can't just leave it in front of the house at home to deteriorate. I need hard cash for the rest of this year's fees. Lord show me your answer. Did you not want me here in the first place?'

THE CAR DIDN'T DETERIORATE, it disintegrated! Neighbours began to protest at the junk heap. A well intentioned relative tried to make it run, took its engine apart and then left it because he could not put Humpty Dumpty together again. Parents wrote in distress and finally I wrote asking them to sell it for junk. It was a total loss and a very bitter lesson in stewardship. Had the Lord got me into the Bible college on the unfulfilled promise of a Christian friend, only to leave me high and financially dry?

The ready answer of some of the fellows in the college did not impress me either. Living by faith, they called it. They made it known to sponsors and good friends of the college who offered them hospitality, that they were living by faith, which to my mind was tantamount to saying they expected a hand-out. They might just as well have worn a begging bowl around their necks. Since then I have come to realise there are more subtle ways of conveying the same impression and I am sure that I have not been guiltless.

The Lord's answer to my prayer gave me some practical lessons in stewardship, met my financial needs and gave me some much needed physical exercise. I had had the necessary amount for the down payment to enter the college course but that was all. While I was working, paying off the car had taken a lot of my stipend. However, being a carpenter by trade it was not difficult to find part-time work on the one free day at college and this, with care, provided sufficient to pay the rest of the term's fees. Then during the holidays I was able to find work of the same nature to help in the next year's fees. During the two-year course, I had only one gift from a Christian friend and it was only enough to buy some flowers to send home to mother. The gift was so unprecedented, the first of its kind in my experience, that it seemed like the precious water that David's courageous men had got for him at the hazardous risk of going through enemy lines. He had poured it on the ground. I could not get myself to spend it on any of the many things I needed and besides, I had been long enough away from home to know just what a wonderful mother I had, and so I ordered flowers to be delivered to her from a shop in my home city.

The Lord obviously led when it came to part-time work, for the people for whom I worked — shoring up their houses and renewing foundations and the like — became very dear friends who not only paid me handsomely on the spot, but, in one case, continued to send gifts from time to time all through the years.

There must have been many fellow students in the college who were living by faith in sincerity and having their needs met in various ways. That I did not hear the details is no proof that it did not happen. For me, at the time, it seemed that I was living on a lower spiritual plane, even though I was critical of those who made their needs known indirectly. I could not deny the fact that the Lord was meeting my financial needs in very pleasant ways indeed. I needed the exercise besides the lasting friendships. But to live by faith still somehow meant to me that needs should be supplied as they were with the tired prophet who wakened to find that the birds had brought his breakfast. Or it meant a Muller who could just remind his Heavenly Father of the needs of his orphans and not be surprised when food or money arrived just in time for the next meal. That the Lord should supply suitable work seemed to be hardly a spiritual kind of answer to my faith — or was it just lack of faith that made it necessary?

Upon graduation from college, I sold my bicycle and thus had enough to get home to the other end of the country. Very soon there came an invitation to help with a beach mission nearby. I demurred because I did not have the cash to pay my own expenses as was necessary with these teams. The leader however eventually persuaded me to join them, assuring me that the need would somehow be met. During the mission, a fellow Bible college student visited the team and gave me a gift of half my financial needs. He could not have known that I had any needs. Towards the end of the mission someone else, also outside the team and therefore ignorant of my needs, gave me the exact sum necessary to make up the deficit in the expenses. It was a delightful experience of seeing the Lord prompt people to share of their substance. Equally delightful because the answer to my needs came from totally unexpected sources. I began to see a principle in all this, for I was not now in the position to be able to meet my need by physical labour. The financial need was urgent and not of my concocting. I was only there by invitation and with a real sense that the Lord was in this request. And later this proved to be so, for I became a pioneer for work for this kind of children's evangelism in a later period of time and this was my introduction. Further, the answer to my needs did not come from another member of the team. Humanly speaking, I might have expected the leader to drop an appropriate hint in the ears of other members who might be able to help. All this assured me that if the Lord was leading me into some work of His choice for me then I could trust Him completely to arrange for my finances and prompt His own people to give to meet my real needs. If, on the other hand, He knew there was some reason why I should 'work' for financial returns while serving Him, then I could expect Him to lead me to the work that best suited my situation.

Time came when it was imperative that Betty and I had

housing of our own for the work that the Lord had given us in Japan. We looked at houses for rent or sale and found them both unsuitable and ridiculously expensive. We were led quite amazingly to a plot of land on top of a hill that had been cleared for building and the very day we signed the contract for the section, not only the most explicit promises were given us from the Word of God assuring us to go ahead, but a gift of $100.00 came 'out of the blue'. About the same time we heard of old lumber available from buildings demolished by a missionary and everything pointed to the fact that my building experience in New Zealand was now going to be necessary in building my own house in Japan.

I could have walked around this vacant section and claimed it by faith, and with it, all the money necessary to get a carpenter to build it completely for us, thus saving both my energy and time for other more spiritual things. As it worked out, sufficient funds were in hand for me to get a Japanese carpenter to put up the frame in a way that is specially suitable for housing here and is different from anything I knew, and then I was able to carry on and finish the house off. The cash came in, bit by bit, as we laboured.

The fact that a missionary would 'stoop' to manual labour, I later discovered, carried a message of peculiar and needed import for the Japanese. One physician friend visited us while the building was still being finished on the inside. He was helping us with language study while we helped him prepare for study overseas. When he heard me take up my tools immediately after going through a sermon for correction with him, he remarked to Betty that I seemed to have spiritual things and material things all mixed up in my life.

The tendency here is for preachers to be looked upon as a professional white-collar class — a priestly group who do not soil their hands. The idea does not stem from the Bible but from a class-conscious society. Later we spent much time and energy in the building of a camp site for which we had received building materials at little cost. What was needed was the labour of putting them together. An elderly Christian in the neighbourhood remarked that if it were not for me, the other missionaries would just have to believe for the money to get the buildings put up by national car- penters. As it was, I had a team of missionaries and Japanese pastors who were members of our organisation, working together on the scheme. Was my determination to work within the limits of our existing cash resources and with the materials to hand, a hindrance to faith? To me, it was just part of the life of faith. Churches were to be built elsewhere by national carpenters and with funds that had come to hand for interest-free loans for the purpose. When time and energy and know-how are all fully and needfully occupied with some other work of higher priority, then I can expect the Lord to supply money and men for any manual labour of that nature, but the Lord obviously knows what honest labour can do for a team of several nationalities who, as missionaries, get too little exercise in any case. One of those national pastors recently, when talking about training for missionary work, remarked on how beneficial it had been for nationals and foreigners to work together in manual labour. He said, 'we really come to know each other that way.'

The relation of faith to honest labour has its poignant side when it comes to discussions with some who think that be- cause they have been called to serve the Lord 'full time' it would be back-sliding to earn money in any way. One pastor once told me that if all funds were cut off, he would starve rather than work. I wish it had been Paul who was sitting beside him when he said that! Not all pastors share the same view, for I know of one who taught English to support him- self during the early days of pioneer church building. Another who was also a qualified engineer drew a sub- stantial salary from the firm he worked for, put it all into the hands of the church treasurer and then received from the church a salary that was less than he collected from the firm. No doubt in his thinking this enabled him to retain his special status as a spiritual leader and at the same time would encourage other members of the tiny congregation to give sacrificially.

It is profitable to recall Paul's attitude to manual labour, for if anyone needed to be free from ordinary work in order to exploit his great gift as an evangelist, and a travelling one at that, it was he. But in I Corinthians 4:12, he says, 'we labour working with our own hands . . .' Then in chapter 9, he argues for the right of Apostles and evangelists and all leaders in spiritual things to be supported financially by the Christians to whom they minister, but adds in verse 6, 'or is it only Barnabas and I who have no right to refrain from working for a living?'

The question is obviously rhetorical and points out the fact that the general rule is that financial support should be available for Christian leaders. But it was a right which Paul was willing to forgo as far as the Corinthians were concerned. Comparing this passage with that of chapters eight and nine in the second letter, it would appear that the Corinthian believers were singularly slow in the grace of giving and Paul compared them unfavourably with other, poorer Christians who gave so readily and sacrificially. No doubt he felt that his refusal to avail himself of their small and reluctant contributions and at the same time to work to support himself would do something to stir their conscience to give more, even if he was not the beneficiary!

Then, if we compare these passages with Acts 18:1, we notice that it was at Corinth that Paul met up with Aquila and Priscilla who, like him, were tent-makers and they laboured together. We can imagine that Paul merely helped them in what was already a well-established tent-making industry where they supplied all the tools. But the friendship thus established was to be one of the precious things in Paul's life. The resulting deeper spiritual life of the young couple paid off in ministry to others.

Paul's attitude was echoed by Carey the father of modern missions who lived to preach the Gospel but 'cobbled shoes to pay expenses'. There are quite a number who today follow in their train. Missionaries can only get into some countries as technicians or teachers and have to spend much of their time at their secular calling. But their purpose is primarily to win nationals to the Saviour.

For years I have had no need of regular employment of such a nature, for Japan is a singularly easy country to enter and to find opportunities for spiritual service. It is also a country where specialists in the teaching of English can find ready employment in colleges and big business houses and there exploit these teaching positions as a means of making contacts for Christ. We long for more dedicated Christians of this calibre who have the faith that they will find the most strategic positions. There are plenty of opportunities for the exercise of faith even if financial needs seem to be so abundantly met thereby.

5

Faith's Obedience

30 January 1950

'Returned tonight from talking to ... about my call to Japan as a missionary. Am I stymied! There is no one whose opinion I value more highly. I owe so much to him. I guess what I had to say about going was not all that convincing. So he suggests that I go into Christian work at home. Perhaps he thinks at my age there is little hope of my getting the language. If he knew how low my Varsity marks were he would be even surer that I shouldn't go.'

THAT NIGHT BEFORE RETIRING, I turned to the passage in the Bible that was my portion for the evening and found myself reading the story of Abram's call to leave his country and family for Canaan, in Genesis chapter 12. Nothing could have been more appropriate and I took it as no accident that I read it that night. The command to Abram was also the Lord's command to me. Abram commenced his life of faith by an act of obedience, no doubt against all the advice and opposition of his relatives and friends, especially since he was going on a journey that had no clearly defined destination. But, 'by faith Abraham obeyed . . .' (Hebrews 11:8) and it's about the obedience of faith that I want to share some things in this chapter.

The call to go to Japan came as no spectacular emotional experience. It came through no impassioned appeal by a missionary on furlough. Japan, at that time, was just beginning to receive missionaries after the war, not sending them home on furlough. If I recall aright, all I knew was that evangelical student work had begun in post-war Japan and the more I thought about it, the more somehow it seemed to have something to do with me and the fact that I had been working among students in my own country for the previous two years and loving every minute of it. The more I permitted myself to think about students in Japan and my own experience at home, the more I began to feel that there was a meaningful relationship that the Lord had permitted by way of preparation. A. T. Pierson once said that facts are the fingers of God. The facts in this case were: there were great numbers of students in Japan singularly open to new ideas in the aftermath of their country's first defeat; a Christian witness had been started among them; and the Lord had led me into student work in my own country, which of necessity was a ministry of limited duration.

For years I had had a vague sense of call to work overseas. No matter what I did and no matter how satisfying it was, there was always the sense that this was not 'it'. Graduation from Bible college was now ten years in the past. The 1939–45 war had followed with four years in the army as a male nurse, in the Pacific zone fighting the Japanese. The nearest I got to the enemy was to attend the wounds of a Japanese prisoner who had been struck by a falling branch of a tree while trying to escape during the night. Then came the university years and subsequent full-time staff work for the Christian Unions. All these experiences proved to be no wasted time. Much of it involved leadership of an inter-denominational nature, even as unofficial chaplain of a group of Christians who would never have met each other if it had not been for the exigencies of war. The trend in all these years therefore was towards interdenominational work. Someone has rightly said that the call of God is not the impulse of a moment but the trend of a lifetime. With me, it was a matter therefore of continuing to say 'yes' to the trend. However, when it comes to going abroad as a missionary, naturally there are some big adjustments involved.

I wanted to be sure that the thoughts I was entertaining and the growing conviction I had about work in Japan were *not* just the impulse of a moment and so sought a friend's advice. Later, he came to fully acquiesce in that conviction. The opposition of others was understandable. Unconverted relatives and spiritually dull churchmen, whose patriotism had watered down their sense of moral responsibility, could think of nothing but the atrocities perpetrated by the Japanese during the war. It never occurred to them that if we had taken the Gospel to them more readily in the past, there might never have been a war to demonstrate just how desperately they did need the Gospel.

As I knelt by my bed that night feeling that God's command to Abram was now a command reiterated for my sake, I knew I had to say yes and leave the consequences of obedience to Him. Since then, there have been other times of special crisis when the Bible portion that fell to that particular day in the systematic readings through the year was singularly apt — indeed, all too appropriate to be a coincidence. So much has this been the case that at the beginning of the year when I am thinking about what Bible reading method to adopt for the year, I have occasionally wondered whether the choice made then is going to affect the pertinency of the Bible passage on the day of any coming crisis! The daily Christian life is not a series of crises of course, nor is it necessary or usual for us to have the apt Bible verse before we can make any moral decision. In most things, daily Bible reading conditions our minds and hearts for instant or delayed reaction consistent with God's will. We begin to think God's thoughts after Him.

I recall the night when the divine intervention of a telegram changed the whole course of my life. After graduation from Bible college and some subsequent Christian service, there was increasing pressure to commit myself to a life work. Just at that time, an opening for work occurred that was most attractive to me and for which many gave willing endorsement. The application was made, but it was finally decided to make no appointments at the time.

I was puzzled. I continued in prayer, however, but at the same time the urge for some action was upon me and when another position for something of the same nature occurred, I asked for the papers. These had to be filled in by a certain deadline and as I did not have real assurance that this was of the Lord I waited till the very last night, trusting that some token one way or the other would give indubitable evidence of His will. I recall actually scrutinising the papers again, still reluctant to fill them in, when the telephone rang. It was a telegram. The substance was to the effect that I was being asked to consider Christian work among students as a staff worker.

I was flabbergasted. Finding it rather difficult to believe that this might be the hoped-for, eleventh-hour intervention of the Lord, I rang up a fellow student from the university where I had been studying and who had actually once mooted the possibility of such a position to me. I now wondered if there had been some well-intentioned work behind the scenes to help the Lord and me at the same time! My friend was party to nothing of the kind, but rejoiced in the request that had been made. With some more assurance that this was of Him, I turned to my reading for the night and it proved to be the passage in Acts 16:1–10, where Paul had twice been restrained by the Holy Spirit from a certain course of action and then while waiting, no doubt in some bewilderment, the vision came from Troas that opened the door of Europe to the Gospel. The twofold restraint and then the last moment intervention seemed to be so akin to my own experience in broad outline that my increasing feelings of utter incapacity for such a task were overwhelmed by the conviction that this was indeed of God.

I later learned that on that same night the executive officers of the movement were meeting to pray about this very appointment many miles away and my name was broached, only to be laid aside because of some knowledge of the previously mentioned applications. Decision was made to go ahead in contacting me however, and then one of them said, 'Well, let's send a telegram now!' Who prompted him to suggest that? Surely the very One who would not have us in a torment of uncertainty, and who well knew that again and again in the future I would need to look back to the fact of guidance that showed He could engineer circumstances when and where it was needed.

Now to some, all this may seem a very fanciful way of knowing the will of God and a very haphazard basis for obedience. I myself have been critical of methods that involved the pulling of Bible promises out of a box of such portions that someone has arbitrarily gathered together for the purpose. Sometimes quite far-reaching decisions have been made upon the basis of such a choice and taken as the will of God. It is possible of course that if someone is shut up by culture and tradition to that method then the Lord confines Himself to the limitations imposed upon Him in that way.

For myself, the Word of God has come as confirmation to some step already suggested in some other way. It has been, to use the promise in Isaiah 30:21, a word behind us, in our ears, saying, 'this is the way, walk in it'. We have had to step out in some direction believing it to be, or at least, hoping it to be the Lord's will for us, and then the Word comes to us as we read it in the regular portion for the day, perhaps out of context, but with specially apt meaning to the present situation, and we get assurance that this is indeed the path of God's choosing.

Sometimes, as with Abram, all we get is the command to go, or, as in his case, to leave his present household and occupation and set out with the assurance that the ultimate destination will only be revealed to him as he obeys and goes forward. Often there is a progressive unfolding of his purposes for us and it is part of the discipline of faith that we move forward under sealed orders, with directions as to the next step only available after we have taken the first.

This was certainly true of a friend of ours who had a very good position as harbour pilot. As a keen Christian, he became increasingly restive under the conditions of labour and unethical practices that he could not condone. Eventually, he felt led to resign his post, to the amazement of the Harbour Master, especially as he had no like position to go to, certainly no position of any advance at all. He felt constrained to go to an inland town of very limited population and where there was no real evangelical witness. At first he had great difficulty finding employment and eventually took a position as a gardener and caretaker for one of the schools. However, this left him free to engage in a kind of Christian work for which he and his wife are specially gifted. Today, there is not only a warm-hearted evangelical witness in the town but their home is becoming a place to which needy folk come from great distances to be blessed.

I have come to see that faith in the Biblical sense is not just a feeling of confidence in God and therefore a committal of oneself to Him. It is all that, but it must involve what Paul at the beginning and ending of his letter to the Romans calls 'the obedience of faith' (Romans 1:5; 16:26). Obedience expresses faith.

Take my salvation experience as an example. I am, in the Bible, commanded to believe on the Lord Jesus Christ (Acts 16:31). I am not asked if I would like to believe. I am not asked to 'decide for Christ', as though I was going to do the Lord the honour of choosing Him in preference to other contestants for my favour. That is not a biblical way of challenging anyone to get right with God. I am commanded to obey the Gospel (2 Thess. 1:8) and disobedience according to the immediate context, results in 'eternal destruction'.

Now the Gospel is good news. How do we obey good news? We trust it to *be* good news. And that is part of the experience of faith. But it also implies a response involving the will. An example would be for us to be wakened at night by the smell of smoke and cries from the street that the hotel has caught fire. We are four stories up and the bottom floors are all ablaze. We rush to the windows and find to our great relief that the firemen have a canvas spread below and we are being ordered to jump from the window and be caught. The good news is that there is a way of escape from incineration. But if we refuse to believe there *is* a fire, and then refuse the offer of help or refuse to trust ourselves to the fall into the professionally held canvas below, we suffer the results of disobedience. In that case, no one can help the one who both refuses to help himself and refuses the help that is proffered. Unbelief and disobedience similarly are often linked in the one experience of rejection of the Gospel, the good news about salvation through the Lord Jesus Christ.

In Mark chapter 3, verses one to five, there is an incident recorded from among the miracles of our Lord that illustrates the obedience of faith. Jesus faced a man with a withered hand and (verse 5) commanded him to stretch it out. Humanly speaking, this was quite impossible, but the man obviously did not think that the Lord was mocking him. In actual fact, the Lord could have healed the man directly with no action of the man's will in the matter at all. This was certainly the case with many of the miracles where because of demonic possession or sickness or death, those to be healed were not able to respond to the Lord normally. In all other cases recorded in the Gospels (except that of Luke 8:42–48 where the response was temporarily hidden) the Lord sought to elicit some response before the healing took place.

In the case of the man with the withered hand, the Lord challenged him to an act of faith that involved the will. The man himself must have looked upon the command as something he could now do, simply because of the One who commanded it. Was it just the Lord's presence, the indefinable but absolute authority — the very look perhaps? Was it confidence based upon the testimony of so many who had been similarly healed? There is nothing in the record to satisfy the psychologically curious, because all we know is that the man willed to do the impossible. The miracle itself must have taken place in the very process of the man obeying — not before — or no voluntary act of the will would have been necessary and the Lord's command would have been mere play-acting for the effect.

Similarly, in the life of faith, sometimes the Lord commands us to do something that humanly speaking seems impossible. We obey, not because there is no alternative or because we are mere spiritual robots who can't demur. In actual fact, there may be a long battle before we say yes. But either immediately, or eventually, we obey because we trust the One who issued the command. We know, even if we have only been a short time on the walk of faith, that the Lord only commands us to free us from things that fetter us. He does not order us around just for the joy of being obeyed and showing us who is boss — in case we had forgotten. Our faith is exercised for the simple reason that we cannot imagine ourselves doing the thing we are asked to do. For this reason we know that unless the Lord supplies the power to will as well as the power to do, we are just going to look very foolish indeed. Yet, the Lord asks us to act in faith, that just as He commands, so we shall be able to do. In this way, His own power is demonstrated and eventually, the full reason is also given and rejoiced in.

The initial call to go overseas as a missionary can be, for some, an impossible command. The physical difficulties seem insurmountable. The human ties, like Abram with Terah and Lot, are too clinging. Our own spiritual impetus has withered through some foolishness and fleshly conduct as a Christian and we hardly dare to think the Lord could yet use us for His glory at home, never mind overseas. But the Lord says 'Go' and we go, because we trust. And that can be the beginning of a lifetime of proving that every command of His is for our blessing.

6

Faith's Mode of Operation

20 February 1950

'*A wonderful letter from . . . today. He writes that if I go out to Japan on my own, then he and a wealthy Christian friend will stand by me financially. He writes that if I go out with a missionary society then I will not have the freedom to work among students as I feel led. I will not be able to exercise the gifts that God has given me. Sounds like common sense to me. And just think — not a financial worry in the world! Isn't that marvellous?*'

THAT WAS MY SPONTANEOUS, very natural and immediate response to the kindness of my friends. However, after more time to think and pray it through, I could get no peace about the offer and declined it. The subsequent twenty-four years on the mission field have now furnished me with the reasons why I was led to do what must have seemed a very foolish thing. I am not sure if I felt foolish about it, but I am glad I did not consult others on an issue like this.

Eventually I applied to a society that very specifically made no promise of any financial support at all. All they promised to do was to forward intact any gifts that came for me through their office and also to share with me from funds that were sent into the mission for general disbursement when personal gifts were inadequate. They made it very clear that the mission was only the channel and never the source of my income. I was urged to look to the Lord alone.

If I was indeed called of the Lord for overseas service then I together with the mission leaders, could look to the Lord to give an initial seal by the supply of the travel expenses to get to the field, and then the continuing and varying supply needed through the years that would follow. Interestingly enough, one of the friends mentioned above did not lose his interest by my joining a missionary society and continued to be a regular donor. Six months after I arrived in Japan, I was seconded to a Christian student movement for whom I have been a staff worker ever since.

If this chapter needs to have any particular theme it will be in terms of 'faith alone' and I want to enumerate some of the blessings of being shut up to the Lord alone.

To Hudson Taylor there seemed to be no alternative. At one time, because of the incapacity of the home secretaries of the Chinese Evangelisation Society, continued association was no longer bearable and he, in far away China, resigned. He felt safer with God alone. C. T. Studd faced a similar imperative. No doctor would recommend him for the foreign field, least of all for darkest Africa, the white man's grave. The small committee that had been formed to back him promptly resigned when they received the doctor's report, for he was already a veteran of missions on two continents and fifty years of age. They would have nothing further to do with such a mad-cap scheme! His wife was sick and there was no support from local churches, yet he had the assurance to declare publicly that he would sail, when as yet he did not have enough to make a deposit on his ticket. The next day a gift came, sufficient for that very purpose, and the rest followed because he was simply being obedient to the One Who loves to create things out of nothing, and Who alone has the right to give commands with which we see no human hope of complying. If He commands the impossible, then it is also up to Him to enable.

Because men like Hudson Taylor and C. T. Studd and others like them have based their policy on the will of God and what they believe to be commanded rather than on the changeable factor of money in hand, despite world wars, or recessions in world markets, missionaries have gone to foreign fields with the Gospel when organisations that were tied to a budget were speaking of decided retrenchment.

The missionary committed to the life of faith is not dependent upon his home church even if they promise him full support. He is not dependent upon his particular missionary society even though he has many reasons to be grateful for

all that it means to have its helpful representation and organised prayer fellowship. One of the missionary's tasks is to
bear witness to the church at large that the Lord is still
working miracles of supply, and he has to maintain the deli-
cate balance of making no appeals of a personal nature even
by implication, but at the same time, testifying to the way
the Lord does honour His own promises. I confess that I
have not always been able to maintain that balance. Even as
missionaries abroad, committed to a programme that stipu-
lates that no appeal be made for funds we can write a prayer
letter that says volumes between the lines. The missionary's
support may thereby increase considerably, but it is doubtful if our usefulness consequently will be extended.

Granted we are subjected to such subtle temptations, and
on occasion suffer from some degree of spiritual double
sightedness, but on the other hand, the missionary who is
sincerely looking to the Lord alone for the supply of his
needs has some decided advantages.

It is easier to preserve the single eye and the undivided
heart when the Lord's service is not tinged by any possible
monetary motive, or affected by the faithfulness or un-
faithfulness of other people's giving . . . I know missionaries
being cajoled into some action, or restrained from another,
by the threatened manipulation of support funds. Foreign
Boards have not been above threatening national churches
with the cessation of further foreign support if they did not
toe the line of the home church's policy.

The missionary who is not living and working on a budget
or assured salary system is more likely to look to the Lord
for His direct will in any new measure that involves the
outlay of funds from abroad, assuring himself that if the
methods contemplated, or the burden of his heart is indeed
from the Lord, then in His time the funds will surely be
supplied as a confirmatory seal. Till that 'cloud' moves, then
it is highest wisdom to wait.

Critics of this approach will remark that people are only
too ready to give to some worthy project, and the home

church is the poorer for lack of opportunity if we do not make the needs known. There is a measure of truth in this, and it is obvious enough that organisations that make their needs known seem to get more. It is equally true that some methods adopted on the foreign fields because of large financial resources, do not give the appearance of being easily absorbed into the life of the local churches. They remain what the Japanese call 'bata kusai', i.e., they retain that distinctly buttery, greasy smell of the West.

Christians in the home churches do not always have the discernment necessary to see the kind of stewardship that will most benefit a foreign church, and are, therefore, easily subject to appeals that are positive, tangible, and that will apparently yield quick returns. One organisation has attracted attention by promising so many souls won for so many dollars — as simple as that!

Sadly enough, rather than give systematically to help missionaries spend their whole lives among a foreign people for the Gospel's sake, many Christians at home are more likely to give, even generously, and certainly spasmodically on impulse, to a very pointed and perhaps emotional appeal.

There is nothing unscriptural about appealing for funds. Paul did it, though it will be noticed that he did not appeal for himself, and took special pains to see that people knew that he did not get a 'commission' out of the money collected for the poor saints of Jerusalem. He went to considerable trouble to avoid any appearance of covetousness, and though he did not fail to express a touching gratitude for the gifts he did receive, he was quite willing to labour with his hands rather than be dependent upon the young church.

It must also be said that the missionary at home or abroad who is living 'by faith' is not necessarily, for that reason alone, living on any higher spiritual plane than the one who has the 'assured' income. Spiritual priggishness and a mercenary attitude — downright worldliness in fact — are possible in either state. The missionary called to a life of no promised support can, if not careful, give way to covetousness and a possessiveness of the things he does possess that is pathetically akin to the spirit of the age. The missionary living on an 'assured' income can, with care, still be independent of things in spirit, though he may not seem to have such frequent opportunities to exercise faith.

We have to settle in our minds, once and for all, that the presence or absence of a surplus of money has little or nothing to do with being in the Lord's will. Our essential ministry is not dependent upon the amount of cash we have in hand. It costs nothing to talk and pray! Indeed, if apostolic example has any bearing on the matter, Paul's description of a missionary in 1 Corinthians 4:8–17 and 11 Corinthians 6:3–10 should make some of us feel very ashamed indeed — 'faith' missionaries included! Certain it is that the more lightly we can sit to possessions, the more effectively we can demonstrate to Christians and the world in a new culture that our essential treasure and our citizenship is not in this world at all. The 'faith' missionary may have more opportunity for this kind of demonstration — and is all the richer for it.

Some have argued that no society worthy of the name of Christian has the right to send young people to the ends of the earth without positive assurance of their needs being adequately met. For the 'faith' mission to do anything else, however, would be to veto one purpose of its existence. The missionary's faith must rest in God alone — absolutely. He is not being sent abroad as a servant of a foreign institution, nor does he join any one mission society because it has the reputation for rewarding its members well, can pull financial strings in influential places, and provide a fat retiring allowance. Unless the prospective missionary has a deep and settled conviction that he is being sent abroad by the Lord Himself, then no matter what society he joins he is going to be a source of irritation; a blot instead of a blessing. He will become obsessed with second causes for every problem he faces, and in any time of lack, or other testing, he will become critical of the society as such, its propaganda or lack of it, and, not least, his fellow workers.

This mission is wise to promise nothing, except to stand with him in faith that the Lord of the Harvest will supply all that he needs. 'God's work done in God's way will never lack God's supply,' is the caption wrought out of hard but triumphant experience in the lives of many missionaries abroad.

There are missions and missions. A prospective candidate should carefully study the history, doctrine, and present practices of any society working in the field to which he feels called, and with whom he wishes to associate himself. Some of the larger societies provide a period of orientation in their home headquarters to enable candidates to become acquainted with the society more closely, for both he and the society need to be fully assured that they are called to work together before he leaves for another country.

A mission society is made up of very human people, and its home personnel can conceivably let a missionary down. The flow of funds to the field can be affected by poor representation or adverse criticism of the home personnel. But returning missionaries have also been known to act very unwisely, and the whole society come under criticism because of it. Unfortunately, even Christian people are apt to label a whole society by the reputation of one of its members. Missionaries who have thus suffered from vacillating public opinion, and perhaps the loss of their supporters through death and other causes, have been able to testify that if their eyes are unto the Lord alone, when the source of supply dries up in one place, it miraculously opens in another. F. B. Meyer has said that the Lord has His cupboards in very strange places at times!

One 'cupboard' that is not so surprising is the team on the field. The Lord often meets the needs of one member of the team through the sacrificial giving of other members of the team. This is not necessarily because we live close together, see each other often and are therefore cognisant of each other's physical needs. In times of special crisis as in sickness and the like, naturally that is so, but most of the time the needs are not known and the Lord prompts individuals to share of their substance.

Our team in Japan is international with missionaries from nine different countries. The amount of funds coming from the respective countries tends to vary considerably and is usually constant in its quantity. We have a pool system whereby a certain sum is agreed upon as a necessity for everyone to maintain a healthy standard of living. This sum may vary from month to month according to the funds available, but expenses such as rents and heating and lighting, etc., have to be paid as legitimate and necessary debts. Now it would have been simple for the treasurer if we had decided upon a certain percentage to be taken from all funds coming into the country from abroad and for this to be put into the pool to cover these expenses and then the rest to go to the individuals concerned. However, it was felt that the principle of voluntary sharing was so vital to real fellowship that we decided to leave it to the individual to decide freely each month how much to put in towards the general expenses. For this reason, each missionary receives all the funds sent to him from his home country and then it is up to him to ask the Lord how much he should allocate. Under a percentage system, someone with large sums available would naturally have to put in a large amount, and anyone with less would put in less. This ordinarily would be the fairest and the simplest way of doing it, but it would then rob the fellowship of its spontaneity, and individuals of possible hidden sacrifices.

Another positive factor has been the attitude of the team at the home end. They are dedicated to the task of sending missionaries abroad and are our encouragement in every way. For this reason, they like ourselves receive no stated salary. They take nothing from funds that come in earmarked for overseas work or personnel. They have to look to the Lord themselves for the supply of their every need, and I often think that folk working away in some mission headquarters like this, who will not be looked upon as missionaries by the general Christian public and apparently not in any financial need, have a more active faith than we do. Most folk imagine that home staff of missionary societies are paid from general funds and cannot imagine staff having to look to the Lord for funds specifically designated for them. But you can imagine what this does for members of the team abroad. We know the home staff are absolutely one with us and are willing to sacrifice what in many cases can be lucrative positions in business to be able to serve the Lord in this way.

No real team spirit is possible without mutual sacrifices. This is another of the reasons why I am glad the Lord led me to join a team or missionary society, for the independent missionary is in grave danger of not only being a law to himself but also an end in himself. We have proved that if we live to give, then the Lord will provide us with more of the wherewithal to give.

7

Faith's Relaxation

20 June 1950

'On the ship tonight. Grateful for the version of Isaiah 26:3 that reads, "Thou dost keep him in perfect peace, whose imagination stops at Thee . . ." Thank you for that Lord. I'm afraid my imagination ran riot today — worse than it ever did in war time.'

THE OCCASION WAS MY departure from New Zealand for Australia, the first leg of my journey to Japan as a missionary. I had already been overseas in the Pacific region as a medical orderly in the Army, but somehow this journey, with far less physical danger attending it, played on my all-too-vivid imagination and I was fearful and apprehensive to an absurd degree. In the army, there was little sense of personal commitment or responsibility. You did what you were told, especially in my humble rank, and you were not going abroad with any spontaneous sense of Mission — at least I wasn't. There was the possibility of death of course, though no doubt we fondly imagined that as medics we were not going to be breasting any bayonet charges. Death besides was still too far off. But this going abroad as a missionary was something quite different. It was not physical fear, but misgivings as to fitness, and apprehension as to situations that would show you up to be the kind of person you knew deep down you really were but hoped that no one else would find out.

I think the thought that I would be working with or under those who were veterans and whom I presumed to have faith and insight to an extraordinary degree, left me uncertain of myself. At that time, the mission had no H.Q. in New Zealand and I was being sent to the H.Q. in Sydney for a period of six months' orientation into the ways of the mission and for testing as to suitability. Perhaps it was the testing side of it that made me most apprehensive, and that in the hands of 'foreigners'. I was to learn what Mark Twain said whimsically about troubles, that he had had many and most of them had never happened. I had the unhappy capacity of imagining myself in the most devastating situations. In some of these I fondly saw myself behaving with astonishing astuteness and aplomb, but most of them just left me cold, the kind of 'tossing all night' kind of subconscious apprehension. If there was any possibility of a head-on collision between personalities then I was at my worst. It was in this area that I suffered the greatest fears and built my most vulnerable castles in the stormiest clouds.

For this reason, the verse in Isaiah that happened to be in my reading the night I left the shores of New Zealand came with special comfort. My imagination was to stop at God. I did not need to imagine anything beyond what He was going to permit in my life, and if He permitted it as part of His perfect will for me then what cause had I to fear? The subsequent experiences in Sydney proved my fears groundless and I left in December for Japan enriched by the fellowship there.

But we need reminding more often than we need teaching, or certainly as much. Later I found I was still building storm clouds in my imagination and so this chapter has to do with the way the Lord has been teaching and continues to teach me something about *the rest of faith* or the inner calm of faith. I can't find the one word to carry all that it means.

Admittedly, the place of keenest testing has been when the body has aided and abetted the imagination to run amok. I have found that the body, its nervous system, and my own mental attitudes are all so bound up in a bundle of counter-acting relationships that one affects the other profoundly. If I had acted on the shouting or aching voice of vital parts of my body at one time or another, I should have died years ago. After reading the *Reader's Digest* for years, I have a fair idea just where the vital organs are and where one is supposed to ache before a coronary. I have accordingly ached in fair facsimile of what I supposed was the real thing. On one occasion it was so frightening that I visited a doctor, who has what all missionaries need — the most puckish and delightful sense of humour. Before the evening was out I was laughing at myself, for just in the process of sharing things with my good friend, my aches had disappeared.

There are many unnatural features about missionary life that contribute to strain of one kind and another. Some missionaries are so built that they respond to stimuli more than others, the whole nervous system being tuned to pick up every impulse that is available. The nervous system, thus overworked, complains. And some of the nerve ends where the voices of protest can be heard seem to be around vital organs, both in the stomach and around the heart. My doctor friend helped me to talk out the causes of my unrest. Just being assured that I was still very much alive did a lot to remove the fret.

One very natural cause for anxiety was whether or not I was going to master the language. However, I soon found that to worry about it cut my capacity for absorption to an extraordinary degree. I came to see that I could trust the Lord to help me get as much of the language as was needed for the work He wanted me to do. This never meant to me that I would speak 'Turkish like a turkey' or that I was not in for a lot of hard work, but I was able to rest in my heart about the when and the how of getting the language. Part of the 'how' came about through the Lord leading me to live with Japanese most of the time I remained unmarried and thus absorbing it in the best environment for learning any foreign language.

Another opportunity to learn how to relax in the Lord has come with every return to the field after furlough. Before we leave for home, the tempo in activity increases till the last year or so on the field sees us with too many commitments and a major problem in choosing priorities. On one occasion we literally staggered to the ship and the leisurely time on board only served to point up how exhausted we were. However, on return, in view of the fact that much of our work has been with students who have the habit of graduating, we find that many of our contacts have disappeared. We find, for a change, that we are not busy missionaries. We don't look like missionaries, or don't act like some of them anyway. The tendency then is to hunt around feverishly for something to do to justify one's existence, ease one's conscience and look the part. The result is simply a sad professionalism and a frenzy of fruitless activity.

On each return to the field, therefore, I have had to come to the Lord again and commit the days of adjustment to Him and tell Him that I am at His disposal and will wait till He shows where time is to be concentrated and energy to be directed.

We have discovered that Spirit directed service or labour brings its own rest. We don't always remember this to be sure, but we know that the Lord has promised to give us *His* rest if we are bearing *His* burdens. In Matthew 11:28 He first of all asks all who labour to come to Him and then He will give them rest. In the Japanese, it is translated, 'make them to rest'. It is sadly possible for the missionary and presumably the Christian worker at home, to be labouring and heavy laden with work that is self-imposed. Obviously there is a distinction between this and the yoke that He invites us to bear — and a yoke implies heavy work. In bearing His yoke — that is, the burden He gives us and places on our shoulders, the burden that is implicitly part of His plan for us and connected with the burden He Himself has for us — this, He says, will bring rest to our souls. It is lightened because we know He shares it. So we find rest in our labour and we can even relax while running! There is a dramatic difference between the two kinds of labour, both as to lasting results and also in terms of the strain involved.

Then, somewhat in the same vein, I would echo the discovery that Hudson Taylor made after years of fruitful service in Inland China. Despite his prodigious labours — or was it partly because of them — there was a deep sense of lack and a longing for a closer walk with God. There were times of darkness and even of despair. No doubt, in the goodness of the Lord this was all preparation for the change that was to come.

But eventually, through a moving letter from a fellow missionary he came to see that what was needed was . . . 'not a striving to have faith . . . but a looking off to the Faithful One seems all we need; a resting in the Loved One entirely, for time and for eternity.' (*Hudson Taylor's Spiritual Secret*, Dr. and Mrs. Howard Taylor, CIM, London, p. 111). In a very special sense, Christ had become all to him, so that he could be carefree in the midst of the most tremendous pressures. Just to rest in the love of the Lord for Him and to joy in the finished work of Christ; to abide and not to strive after a holiness apart from the Lord Himself, possessing instead His inward holiness, these were some of the precious truths he grasped and he could speak of himself as a new man.

This to me is basic to the life of faith. Problems of financial support and the like are peripheral; they are incidental to the fundamental principle in the daily Christian life. They are related in the sense that one cares less about sources and means for physical support in proportion to the closeness of one's walk with the Lord and the simplicity of one's faith in every other aspect of one's life and ministry.

If we seek first the Kingdom of God and His righteousness, then we can expect the Lord to honour His promises and supply us with all we need, though not necessarily with all we want! We can trust His wisdom to withhold what He must know to be either not good for us or not necessary.

Sometimes we roll our burdens upon the Lord in prayer but we do not maintain an attitude of positive faith, believing that the Lord is now undertaking for us. My recurring temptation is to try to help the Lord out by letting my imagination play around with ideas on how He is going to help us. Mentally, I suggest people whom I think would be the logical ones to help us, or whom He could prompt to help us, usually because they are the ones who have helped us before. But one of the special delights of the life of faith, and perhaps specially of imperfect faith, is the Lord's capacity for giving us surprises. I love to think of Him as the 'Lord of Hosts', obviously with 'hosts' of ways of doing things for us.

8

Faith's Patience

9 January 1955

'Today I wrote to Betty asking her to become my wife. Sent the letter to Canada tonight. Strange that the conviction that it was the fullness of God's time for us both came to me while walking the hills of Kobe studying Japanese!'

BETTY AND I HAD met in 1951. At first sight, even before we were formally introduced, I had the strangest sense of affinity, as though we were needed together to make up one whole person; as though we had always belonged but now we had bumped into one another. Her first sight of me was the back of my bald head!

I was thirty-five and she thirty-one. We began to correspond, for ordinarily we were separated by over 500 miles and were members of different mission organisations. However, we could get no assurance to go ahead with marriage and eventually correspondence ceased. In my life, other ideas were entertained and for Betty, there was responsibility in mission leadership that could not lightly be turned aside. For both of us, it proved to be a time when the Lord was testing our motives and allegiance to Himself. Could we say from our hearts that the Lord Jesus was supreme in our affections? Did we know that Christ could satisfy us absolutely whether we married or not? Would the Lord continue to be the ruling and governing factor in our married lives, if we were to marry? We have realised that only in that sense is marriage safe and the real joys of married life preserved. Married life then is a permanent relationship between three persons, the Lord always having the deciding vote and to be consulted in everything, separately and together.

Betty was by this time in Canada having been whisked home because of the fatal illness of her guardian aunt. Her reply did not come till March the 17th. She still felt God was calling her to walk alone. I have a note in my diary which reads, 'This closes another chapter in the difficult path home to the land where every desire shall be transformed with the glory of His presence.' However, I wrote again on March the 27th with growing assurance that the chapter was not closed. In the meantime, Betty had herself asked the Lord that if this thing was of Him, then I would be constrained to write again before the end of the month. My letter arrived on the 31st of March!

She received it as she was leaving for a meeting and read it en route to the train. On the train she took out her Bible and found in her passage the verse, 'This thing is from Me . . .' At the station on arrival, she pulled out a tract from her bag, one of a bunch that she had picked up at random for distribution, and was about to hand it to a lady, when she noticed that the title of the tract was, 'This thing is from Me.' Rather an unusual title for a tract. On the 12th of April I received a reply saying that she would be glad to marry me, and we married on that day, just one year later.

Naturally we had good reason to ask ourselves why we had to wait till I was thirty-nine and Betty thirty-five. The Lord had a work for us each to do singly that we could not have done had we married earlier. I have touched on the matter of heart preparation for marriage itself and our relationship with the Lord in all this, but we also came to see that only as we had really found that the Lord did indeed satisfy us apart from marriage, did we have the right to say to single girls in Japan that they did not have to marry (even non-Christians) to find fulfilment, despite all the advice of well-meaning friends to the contrary and despite all the pressures of a culture that looks upon the unmarried with suspicion and upon the relatives of unmarried daughters with scorn.

For her part, Betty felt that the Lord would have to work

a miracle in Canada for her to get back to Japan because she was now caring for her widowed guardian uncle. But in time, without prompting from her, he voluntarily suggested that she must prepare to go back to Japan and not to worry about him. The Lord wonderfully provided for him. Then later, independently and yet at the same time, we both felt that we should reconsider our relationship and wrote each other so, the letters crossing in mid-air. This was a real puzzle to us both. Things had seemed, at last, to be going swimmingly, but before any official engagement was made public, for some inscrutable reason, we were having to lay the whole thing down again.

Only later did we see the merciful providence in this restraint. If we had announced our engagement at the time, Betty would have had to resign from her mission in order to join mine, and might have had to spend some time in the mission H.Q. in Canada. All this could have delayed our marriage considerably. Besides, it served to give us further assurance as to His will in the following way. We agreed by mail that Betty would not inform me as to the date of her arrival back on the field and if by some other means it worked out that I heard, and that the Lord caused our paths to cross, then we would take it as a sign from the Lord that we should proceed with our marriage. Several months later, it came about that there was to be a staff conference in Tokyo for the student work I was engaged in and I booked my train reservation for the 29th of December. This was a distance of some 400 miles from where I was living. A few days later, I heard through a mutual friend that Betty was due in Yokohama, the nearest port to Tokyo, on the 30th! We were engaged that weekend.

Now you may well ask what all this has to do with the life of faith. It is connected in two different ways. One has to do with the patience of faith in our relationship with God and the other has to do with mutual faith in each other.

The patience of faith (James 1:3) means that we trust the Lord to lead us to the right person for marriage and we trust

Him as to the fullness of His time for the marriage to take place. We have found it wise to obey any check of the spirit, any restraint He suggests in our relationship with others.

We know of many Christians who have been pressured into engagements by well meaning parents or friends. The whole drift of life and thinking in the West is towards an early marriage as though this was at least one area of life that can be taken for granted. As long as one is in love, then little else needs considering, certainly not God. We believe that time should be taken to test the validity of the friendship by plenty of opportunities for wholesome companionship and prayer and fun together in fellowship with others of the same age group. We can trust Him to give abundant signs as to when we should contemplate serious friendship with a view to marriage and we should certainly not appear to be serious about it unless we have that in mind. Paul Little, in his remarks on guidance, points out that the God we know, does not look down from heaven when we are enjoying ourselves to say, 'Now then, cut it out!' The Lord knows how to give real joy that is absolutely unalloyed with no vague misgivings. Married life in His will and in the fullness of His time, next to our relationship with the Saviour Himself, surely is the most joyful experience of all. For this reason I always urge a long friendship, a short engagement and a very long marriage! We happened to start a little late and apart from fun about it, I never urge anyone to wait until they are thirty-nine.

One clear indication as to whether another person is the Lord's choice for a life partner, is whether there is complete trust; confidence based upon respect. This is the mutual faith side of the ideal marriage. In many cases, love so colours one's outlook in these things that confidence is based upon sheer admiration and can become quite unrealistic. Love in the biblical sense, according to Bishop Stephen Neil, is 'the steady direction of the will towards another's lasting good'. Love in the all too common usage of the term, certainly in non-Christian, pagan circles, is merely the exploitation of another's physical attractiveness and the use, especially of the female partner, as a sexual toy.

With most of us, we trust a partner because we love him or her, and that love can have a number of stimulating factors. At the beginning, we may not be greatly concerned with any altruistic promotion of the other person's supreme good. Certainly, the overwhelming desire to possess another person for oneself is just basic to the instinct for procreation and necessary for the preservation and continuation of the human race. As a Christian, I shared in the same basic drives. However, as a Christian, I have found myself influenced also by profound motives that the non-Christian will know nothing about.

I believed that my choice of a partner was next in importance to my choice of the Saviour. I had assurance to believe that if this were so then the Lord would clearly lead me to the one He was preparing for me. For this reason I felt I did not have to go looking for a wife — even at my ripe years — but the Lord would lead me to one with whom I could share the same motives in life and thus be united not just in body but also in every other phase of daily life and planning. For this reason, it seemed to me that such a partner would naturally have identical interests but not necessarily identical hobbies or preferences in music or tastes in diet — though they happen to be the same with us. I was not surprised, therefore, when I got to know Betty a little better to find that so many things about her background and mine were similar, despite the fact that our countries were different.

When it came to mutual trustfulness, we had decided advantages. It was not because we were older than most couples and therefore could be expected to have mature judgment on these things. Surprisingly enough it had to do with the fact that we knew we were both sinners. We knew we could trust one another simply because of the One in whom we both trusted, who Himself could keep us truthful in our remarks to one another. It is because we know the

Lord has guided us together that we know He'll give the solution to selfishness and touchiness and careless wounding words that can afflict the dearest relationship on earth. He is the One who helps us deal with these and other problems when two sinners live together. Marriage is not just confidence in one another but also confidence in the One who brought us together and who keeps us a sensitive co-operating team with Himself. This is why, to me, faith very decidedly has much to do with marriage.

9

Faith's Frustrations

17 October 1958

'*Off to Shikoku tonight for pioneer work among the universities there. Prayed for Betty at lunch time as she had a bad pain in the chest. It left immediately we prayed in Jesus' name that it should go. Must have been an attack of the devil. Asked some student girls to come and stay with Betty while I am absent.*'

BETTY HAD NOT TOLD me of the pain in her chest earlier in the day as she did not want me to cancel the trip for her sake, especially if it was only a passing trouble. By lunch time, however, the pain was so severe that she could no longer hide her distress when we sat down to lunch together. I asked what was wrong and on being told, instead of giving thanks for the food, I prayed that if this thing was permitted of the Lord to prevent a greater tragedy, then we accepted it as a check from Him. But if it was an attack of the devil to prevent me from going to Shikoku, then right then, in Jesus' name, we refused it and bade it be gone. The pain left immediately and when it did return momentarily later in the afternoon, it was of so little consequence that we took the whole incident as an attempt of the devil to thwart what he must have feared was going to be a successful attack on his property on the island. So it proved to be, for the visit marked the beginnings of an evangelical student witness in the colleges there and the first of many visits by ourselves and Japanese staff workers.

Although we both felt quite sure as to the origin of the trouble, naturally enough, I was a little more concerned than usual at the thought of leaving Betty alone, so while I was away we arranged for some students of a local hostel for girls to take turns in coming to stay with Betty overnight. This enabled Betty to get to know the girls and enter into their problems in a way that would not have been possible if I had been there. If Satan was behind this whole attack, as he indeed seemed to be, then he had overstepped himself in two ways on this occasion.

Frustrations in the way of faith? This is not an uncommon experience. Sometimes the devil can be the undoubted cause of the trouble for if a work is of the Lord, then the devil will do all in his power to upset its very inception. Perhaps he has enough wisdom to know when something will contribute to his own downfall and loss of control in other people's lives. Amy Wilson Carmichael tells the story of how the building of the Forest House for the refreshment of workers at Dohnavur met with such harassment. It seemed as if the venture was doomed, there was so much trouble with the workmen and so many unexplainable disasters in so many different ways. They could have taken it to mean that the venture was not of God, but they believed that the vision was of the Lord and so hung on to His promises.

We had the same experience in the building of our own home in Japan. No one could have been surer that the Lord had guided us to this spot on the hill. Gifts had come just when needed. The promises from the Word had been so singularly apt and encouraging as we started out on this major venture of faith — and work. Then, we found that the landowner was notorious for sharp dealing and keeping just within, or slightly beyond, the law. The carpenter we had engaged through his advice to put up the frame of the house also proved to be quite unreliable and if it had not been that I had had building experience, the huge bulge in the front of the house that I could see at a glance, might have remained to be a laughing stock to all who passed. A major beam on one side of the house was short and he covered up the mistake without fixing it. The whole house I later discovered to be leaning out of plumb about two inches towards the south. So much so, that the front door will not remain open. It closes of its own accord. (The lean helps when the typhoons blow from the south!) Sub-contractors made promises to come and finish their work, but I had been foolish enough to listen to some tale of need and paid them before the work was completed. They never came back to finish off their contract. In so many ways, our spirits were harassed and tired and yet today, no one can deny that the Lord has had His hand upon Hebron House for good and the blessing of many. Laughing, when we could laugh we have often said, 'we progress from problem to problem'.

However, there are some frustrations connected with the tests of faith that do not yield such immediate and substantial, visible results. My heart goes out to Paul every time I read of his being left in the Caesarea gaol by Felix (Acts 24:27) just as a diplomatic gesture to the critical Jews. Though the motives of the Governor were mercenary, it did provide an opportunity that Paul would be glad to grasp and use to the full: the opportunity of talking personally to Felix for two years. But the Governor remained unrepentant, using the dedicated apostle as a kind of intellectual and religious sounding board to while away the dull moments of public office. Paul probably expected to be released. He no doubt felt that after all that time, Felix would surely be sympathetic and see that this imprisonment was unreasonable and a travesty of justice.

Paul must have longed to be free and on the road to reach new areas for Christ. He had all the gifts for that ministry but he was kept penned up at the whim of an intellectual dilettante, and thrown an occasional opportunity for preaching, much as one would throw nuts to a monkey in a cage. I can imagine how trying this must have been to a spirit as sensitive and as great as Paul's. Yet, what would have happened to our Bible if Paul had not been incarcerated in prison, not just this once but several times? If there had not been these times of enforced inactivity, I wonder if the prison epistles would ever have been written? How infinitely poorer the church would have been without them!

Many of us know what it means to be a prisoner of circumstance, but in the midst of the natural frustration we can produce our best work. A good example of this is the life of Amy Wilson Carmichael, who originally spent some time in Japan but because of sickness had to leave her fruitful ministry. Later she went to India and began a ministry that was to last fifty-five years without a furlough. At the height of her most useful work in the rescue of children from temple prostitution, she had an accident with a broken ankle and other complications. This deteriorated into what became a chronic illness that kept her inactive for twenty years. Think of it! She, who had been used as an instrument of healing for others, now appeared to be without faith for her own healing. Surely, no one was more needed on her two feet than she in these dangerous missions and in the early days of a growing work among the children.

There was the frustration of getting better of one ailment only to be afflicted with something else. She writes in *Rose from Briar*, p. 49 (S.P.C.K., London), 'After the foot began to mend other troubles came, one after the other, pulling me up just when I seemed as though I might soon begin to walk. As each corner was turned we thought it would be the last, but there was always another.' And so it went on for twenty years. But what light came out of the darkness of that suffering! Her ministry in writing has blessed the church in such a way that one is almost inclined to thank the Lord that she was permitted to suffer — for us.

A good deal less dramatic, but none the less frustrating have been some of our answers to the prayer of faith. A student from Kyoto Imperial University, Japan's second most important, faced me in my study, a picture of despair. He was the leader of the Inter-Varsity Fellowship group on campus, a small group of Christians and seekers in a college of 20,000 students. He said, 'Teacher, I want to resign from leadership. I cannot carry on. Please take over the group yourself.' I tried to find the reason for the collapse of responsibility, worried equally at his obvious slump in faith and at the possibility of the college group fading out after all those years of witness.

What added to my growing concern was not just the fear he himself would drop out of the race, which he did, but that I was being asked to do something on campus which an I.V.F. staff worker should not do. These groups simply must be student led. A staff worker can visit them and teach them if he is invited to do so, but on no account must he appear to be the actual leader or pastor of the group. It was so against all that I had learnt, knew and deeply felt. But what was the alternative? Either go, or have the group fade out entirely?

For some weeks, with very mixed feelings indeed and with an unbroken burden for God to step in, in a way that I could not even imagine, I taught the group. Then, one day, another of the students came to my study and, if anything, gave me a bigger surprise.

'Teacher, from now on I think I should lead the group. I think it would be wise if you didn't even come for a while!'

Now, if it had been one of the regular attenders and one with a sound church life, I would have been delighted. But not this fellow, of all people. *He*, the answer to my prayers? I knew his background too well. True, he had come to the Lord at an I.V.F. Conference and his conversion had seemed real enough. But at the moment, he was the last one I would trust with any responsibility. What could I do? Despair, as much as anything, drove me to consent to his taking the reins.

It was not very long before he began to go to church regularly. Then an amazing thing began to happen. An absolutely unique gift began to make its appearance — certainly unique for Japan and not too conspicuous in the West either. He seemed to have an uncanny capacity to see what needed to be done and to encourage others to do it, the right people too! The result was that even meetings in our own home, which till then we had had to lead and publicise, to our joy he declared were now the responsibility of the students themselves, and he set up a committee to handle them. This remains so to this day.

He has now graduated and works as an engineer. But all his spare time is given to helping the student witness and in a way that again is unique. He has organised cells of support for the national staff in this area and the inspiration of his quiet, but persistent leadership, has resulted in really sacrificial giving on the part of a closely knit team of young graduates. One unmarried graduate gives almost all his salary for this purpose every month. The success of his leadership in this way obviously is going to influence the giving and organisation of the graduate work of I.V.F. for the whole of Japan. He is still a visitor to my study and I often thank the Lord that He brought me to the place where despair had no alternative but to accept the Lord's apparently unpromising answer to my prayers.

Another frustrating experience came on the eve of our departure from England. We had been six months in Great Britain at a mission leaders' conference and for other commitments, and were to make a short ten-day trip to Germany and Switzerland before we took a charter flight from London to Japan.

We had reached Harwich and were about to gather our things together before the train stopped when suddenly there was a keen sense of having forgotten something. The passports! How could we possibly have forgotten them, of all things? True, it had been one of the most hectic days of our lives. Friends came to say a last farewell, even Betty's brother turned up from Canada, and we went from one thing to another with no time for reflection. But how could we have forgotten the passports!

At the port, there was a not too momentary sense of frustration; a lashing out against circumstances and trying to find a scapegoat and blame someone, anyone but self. Often we have been prompted to remember an all important forgotten item for a journey before getting around the bend of the road, so the Lord could have prompted us before we left the Mission H.Q. Why wait till we were about to board the ferry for Europe?

We asked the port officials if we could proceed and they said yes we could board the ferry but could not guarantee we would be permitted to proceed through Holland. It was too big a risk. We began to think that there were so many strange things about this that perhaps the Lord was shutting up our way. In actual fact, as we left the H.Q. and settled down in the train, there had come a strange sense that the coming journey was unreal. We could not believe we were actually leaving the U.K. I had personally looked forward very keenly to the visit to Switzerland particularly as I had always revelled in mountain scenery, and now hoped to see it with my own eyes.

We found a portside pub for the night and also soon discovered that the sheets had not been changed since who knows how many guests before. We got down on our knees and said, 'Lord, we are your confused children. What do you want us to do? Show us clearly and we will obey.' Should we go back and get our passports and leave the next night? It was the logical thing to do but somehow there was a sense of restraint. As we rose from our knees two things impressed themselves on our minds. We decided that we should phone Germany to see if it would be upsetting if our meetings had to be cancelled. The next was to phone the charter flight airlines to see if there were two seats available on an earlier plane to Japan. The answer from Germany was 'No', and from the airlines, 'Yes'. Immediately we determined to go back on this earlier flight, and things began to fall into place. We realised then that the matter of the forgotten passports was only the climax of a series of frustrations in our plans to visit Germany and Switzerland, though we had prayed about our plans and thought we had the Lord's leading. But in faithfulness, he had shut up our way. When we returned to the mission H.Q. and our patiently waiting passports, we found there was substantial reason why we had to be back there for a few days longer. When we got back to Japan there was good reason why we had to be back earlier than planned.

A momentary frustration and fleshly reaction is natural enough, though we have felt the Lord's checks in various ways enough to know it is imperative that we stop and take notice. He could, of course, have prevented us from making any plans for the Continent at all. Had some contingency arisen in others' lives that caused Him to want us to change our plans? That could have ben so, for so it seemed at the time. Certainly the emergencies we had to meet were not in sight when first planning the return trip through Europe. Then again, sometimes we have to be halted in our tracks like Balaam.

The interpretation of the frustrations of life is one of the disciplines of the life of faith. We can trust the Lord implicitly when he seems to contradict Himself and apparently reverse previous guidance He has seemed to give. Sometimes He just has to say, 'What I do thou knowest not now, but thou shalt know hereafter.'

I am sure that Amy Wilson Carmichael felt this way as she left her beloved Japan never to return. She has recorded her misgivings and fears at the time. 'And yet, oh the many many "buts"! What will people say? How strange it will look. Nobody will understand. And then some thoughts that I cannot write down — fears as to unsettlement of all your minds. Then like a swarm of mosquitoes the unkind, misjudging remarks that many would make, and then, hardest of all, again and again fears about those nearest and dearest. Through them all came calmingly the assurance that, as to what hurt most, He would take care of that, and as to others, one must be content to be misjudged. He was.' (*Amy Carmichael of Dohnavur* by Frank Houghton, S.P.C.K., p. 74.) Little did she realise that she was to spend so long in India, do her major work there and love India and serve India as few have done.

It's not what happens to us that counts, so much as what

we do with what happens. It's the interpretation of events that changes their impact on our lives. Faith has no quarrel with Omnipotence and the Omnipotent One has lots of patience with our frustrations.

It has been suggested that it was sickness that shut Paul up to a ministry in Galatia (Gal. 4:15). All that we are told in Acts 16:6 is that he went through the region of Phrygia and Galatia, having been forbidden by the Holy Spirit to speak the word in Asia. Some would doubt if sickness could ever be an instrument in the Lord's hands to get us to the place of His choosing for us or into the ministry where we really belong. All I know is that so many of the Lord's greatly used servants suffer disability in some way or other, that I doubt if we can disallow sickness as an instrument for good in the Lord's hands on some occasions. There are other situations that are equally trying and frustrating to a sensitive spirit, but the Lord knows what to use to keep us in the path of His choosing, as long as we are willing to do His will.

10

Faith's Fleece

20 August 1968

'*A gift came for $50.00 from Mr. —— in New Zealand today. Was Betty delighted! Apparently she had prayed for a gift of that amount from one person as a seal on her going with me to England next year. Looks as if the donor must have been moved to send this about the time that Betty prayed. Must enquire . . .*'

THE MISSION WAS TO have its first worldwide Leaders' Conference in London in April 1969 and the wives were also invited to come. Delegates looked to the Lord for their own travelling expenses for this conference, and so we thought twice about Betty going along 'just for the ride'.

It seemed for a number of reasons it would be helpful if she could accompany me, and so it proved. Without consulting me she asked the Lord to prompt someone to send us a $50.00 gift. She felt that such a large gift would be sufficiently out of the ordinary to warrant it being a sign that she should go with me and a token that the Lord would supply all that was needed for her fare.

We wrote thanking our new friend and told him how this had come as a specific answer to prayer and mentioned the date when Betty had prayed. His reply brought further assurance. He had recently retired and as he had more time for prayer he had written a few months earlier to the Mission headquarters in New Zealand asking for the name of a missionary he could pray for in a specific way. The secretary sent our name, probably because we were from the same city. For years he had given to the Mission's general fund, but had never given personal gifts to any of the missionaries. Then he received a burden to send us a $50.00 personal gift. He had this burden for about a month, probably waiting to make sure it was from the Lord. On July 17th he sat down and wrote the cheque for that amount. That was the day Betty prayed for that amount in Japan! Was it a co-incidence? We felt not. The circumstances warmed our friend's heart — incidentally we had never met — and greatly encouraged us.

This kind of praying is commonly called 'putting out a fleece' because of the way Gideon sought some confirmation from the Lord about a coming battle with Israel's enemies (Judges 6:26–40.) He asked the Lord to make the fleece wet with dew when all the ground around it was dry, and then on another night, for the fleece to be dry and the ground around it wet. Given these phenomenal signs in nature he would take heart for the coming battle. Call this experimental faith, or props to timid faith if you will, but this is a fairly common way of ascertaining the mind of the Lord even today. Actually, in Gideon's case he already knew the mind of the Lord, for there had been express directions as to what he had to do. He simply wanted assurance that the Lord was going to give him victory over the tremendous forces arranged against him. No doubt he thought that if the Lord could work a miracle in nature He could work another in the coming test of strength. The Lord accommodated Himself to His servant's wish.

When it comes to uncertainty as to the Lord's will then a better example can be found in the action taken by Jonathan in 1 Samuel 14. There is a 'may be' in v. 6, for Jonathan is uncertain about the proposed action being of the Lord or not. So, in v. 8, there is the 'If they do this, then we will do that' approach to the situation. Then, in v. 10, 'and this shall be a sign to us . . .' In other words, they were themselves deciding the terms of reference; they were suggesting to the Lord what should be the sign of His approval in the coming venture, though they did not ask for something quite extraneous to the whole scene nor even something of a miraculous nature. It would be somewhat out of the ordinary for their inveterate foe to ask them to come up and join them peaceably and they chose this as extraordinary enough a sign for their purposes. They moved forward with confidence in the face of vastly superior forces, and started a rout among them.

In the New Testament we find no record of anything precisely the same as a means of ascertaining the mind of the Lord, though we cannot always deduce final conclusions from the silences of the Bible. The nearest we come to it is in the choice of Matthias to succeed Judas as the twelfth apostle (Acts 1:26). In this case they cast lots between two men whose names were put forward. They obviously trusted that the Lord would overrule in the way the lot fell to show which of the two was His choice. We are not told exactly what was meant by the casting of lots, but presumably it was something akin to our drawing of straws as children. It was a matter of simple chance. But in the biblical scene they believed that God was Lord of circumstances Who could control men both in their simple reflex actions and in vastly more complex decisions as well. Later, after Pentecost, we notice that the Holy Spirit guided disciples more directly. Acts 13:2 records the Holy Spirit speaking directly to the assembled group in such a way that they knew who was being designated for a certain task. On another occasion (Acts 16:6) they were restrained from action by the Holy Spirit, in this case the initiative being with the Holy Spirit from the beginning.

Today, I am sure it is true to say that many of the Lord's children have sought to ascertain the Lord's mind in some crisis or other by 'putting out a fleece'.

More recently, we had a most difficult decision to make that we knew would profoundly alter our future ministry and place of work. We were invited to take a position of responsibility in another country. The invitation was unanimous and therefore could not lightly be set aside or refused. There were circumstances in our lives and ministry that seemed to indicate that this call was of the Lord. Yet others who knew us better and were more directly concerned with and responsible for our place of work, felt real reservation about this call. Because of this we ourselves became more confused. Personally, quite apart from the opinions of others, we were tossed from assurance at one time, to profound disquiet at other times — most other times, to be frank. Obviously our feelings were quite unreliable. At one moment we were in favour of the move and looked forward to it with some anticipation. The next we were plunged into despair at the thought of all that was involved and the demands that would be made upon our limited abilities. From inner conviction alone we could not trust ourselves to find the Lord's mind over the matter.

For this reason we longed for some sign of the Lord's mind that was outside ourselves: something right outside all the people involved in this decision and yet that could have some bearing on the final choice. Finally, when a decision had to be made, in the nick of time as it were, an invitation came from an entirely unrelated direction, with a plea to help in a similar work in another country. We took this to be the Lord's intervention, and so with some peace of mind declined the first invitation and agreed to pray about and investigate the second. This led to a limited ministry in that country and finally we both were given simultaneously a real assurance from the Lord to return to the country where we now have worked for over twenty years.

On reflection, though it could hardly be called 'putting out a fleece', yet we were shut up to the Lord so to order circumstances that there would be some indubitable sign as to the direction in which He would have us go. We were not suggesting the sign in this case, except in so far as we longed for it to be outside the whole situation that had become too complex for us.

In any seeking of a sign, in any 'putting out of a fleece', there are obvious dangers. Christians can read extraordinary meanings into commonplace happenings. I have been astonished at what some will say is to them the voice of the Lord. Today the emphasis is definitely upon the inner voice, the sensory and the spectacular, so we need biblical and objective guide lines. On furlough, a girl spoke to me saying she felt the Lord was calling her to stop her studies and join a youth organisation to serve the Lord overseas. She was still only fifteen years of age and because she had failed her examinations to get into High School she took this to be the voice of the Lord calling her into full-time service. I had grave doubts about her call. I felt that what she needed was to settle down to a more disciplined life and concentrate upon study for a change. She could become a professional no-hoper, a confirmed drop-out. At the slightest touch of something difficult or beyond her, she would look for an easy way out. This attitude carried over into Christian service would be fatal. Either to raise some personal experience as a sign, or take from some experience an arbitrary 'God-given' signal as to the Lord's mind can be very dangerous indeed.

The Lord has promised to guide the meek in judgment. I believe there are objective indications as to when it is right to 'put out a fleece', but generally speaking it should be the exceptional rather than the usual way of finding the Lord's mind.

11

Faith's Sacrifice

2 June 1973

'Today addressed a meeting of mission leaders in
Sydney. One of the other speakers remarked during the
course of his address, with reference to members of
some other societies, "they live by faith, which means
no money." Should have challenged him on the spot,
but as usual, I'm too slow on the draw. I think of all
the kinds of apt and wise things to say after the opportunity has forever gone for me to say them.'

ON REFLECTION I CAN see that he was partly right. It does mean no money — sometimes. We have yet to experience this personally. In that respect, alongside some other factors, we are not very Apostolic! Paul said to the Philippian Christians that he had learned the secret of facing plenty and hunger, abundance and want (Phil. 4:12). To the Corinthian Christians he confesses to being poor and yet able to make many rich; to having nothing, and yet possessing all things (2 Cor. 6:10). Then the N.E.B. translates verse 5 of the same chapter to read that Paul had known what it meant to be overworked, sleepless and starving. If there is any similarity at all between the evangelistic journeys and church planting ministry of Paul and that of the ministry of modern missionaries, we might presume that at some time and to some degree there would be perhaps an experience of want. At least it should not take us by surprise and bring discredit upon the way of faith, for that is the way Paul lived.

In actual fact, these days it tends to be very much a rare experience. C. T. Studd, the founder of our society, once remarked that he wondered if the Lord was ever going to trust us with poverty! He, himself, gave away a considerable personal fortune for Christ's sake. However, we know of one couple who came right to the end of their financial resources and could afterwards give thanks for the experience. They

ere stationed in a distant part of inland China and reduced
o the last meal. Mail came and with it four letters from the
U.S.A. They naturally expected that the prayed-for financial
deliverance would be in one of these, but were disappointed.
They were distressed, not least because the cook was ready
to go to the market for supplies and they felt it would affect
their testimony before him if they had to confess that the
God they trusted had let them down. Just then a Chinese
colporteur came to the door. They knew him to be very poor
and a true lover of the Lord Jesus. He told them that the
Lord had told him to give them a silver dollar. They were
reluctant to take it but could not refuse in view of the man's
sincerity and their situation. The whole experience was
specially precious to them in that they realised afresh that
the Lord Jesus Himself was the source of their supply and
not rich Christian friends.

For some of us, even though we have never been totally
without money for food, the way of faith has meant little
money, and for that we have also been thankful. The reason
is that sometimes the Lord can speak to us through our
stomachs when we fail to hear Him through our thick ears!
During one period here in Japan, although not really
hungry, there was a time of decided shortage in funds
from abroad. For some time we had been discussing ways
and means of getting the churches and believers more involved in the support of their own spiritual leaders, but little
had been done. We were largely supporting the national
fellow workers from our support funds. This decided lack
forced the issue, and definite steps had to be taken to see that
local churches began to assume their practical responsibilities much more realistically. The funds from
abroad then became buoyant once more.

A large missionary society which is *not* committed to the
principle of making no appeals for funds, also faced a time
of serious need financially. The whole mission was called
together to Tokyo for a time of prayer about this and the
Lord met them in a most unexpected way. There were prob-

lems in their midst that were much more serious than the lack of funds. As they engaged in prayer, the Lord began to speak to married couples who were on the point of separation, and to individual missionaries who were critical of other fellow missionaries. Soon there was such a time of melting in the Lord's presence that the blessing of those times overflowed and many in other societies throughout the country were also touched for good. It is doubtful if it would have been possible to get this widely scattered group together in this special way if the physical need had not been so serious. I know of at least one couple that have never been the same since and presume they can thank the Lord that financial need got them to their knees.

Sometimes we wonder if missionaries would be more fruitful if they *had* less money. We certainly know what happens when there is too much! I would gather that this was one of the reasons for friction between missionaries and Filipino Christian workers that Chandu Ray reports in his July 1972 Cofae letter.

I quote:

Local personnel (evangelists, translators, tribal workers, etc.) do the same work as the foreign personnel but only receive about one-tenth of the salary. The real irritant comes when the foreigners control this low salary of local personnel, at the same time delivering lectures on being 'sacrificial'. Filipinos have a high respect for one who serves the Lord sacrificially, and they are not seeing this kind of sacrifice on the part of the foreigners. The Filipino accuses the missionary of living in plush homes in 'bourgeois communities', having the latest in appliances and equipment and driving in new luxury cars. The missionary says the Filipino is guilty of the same because he wants all those things and will go into debt to get them.

When a Filipino has a complaint against a foreign missionary there is no one he can turn to: no court of appeal. The Filipino has to get along with the foreigner or get out of the organisation. A co-operative programme may look good on paper, but because of the vast economic imbalance (subsidy and salaries) there is no real equality. Often a well trained Filipino hesitates to join a foreign controlled Christian organisation, or will take a job only as a temporary measure.

It stands to reason, human as we are, that we tend to live up to our means. The sad thing is that some Christian work abroad gives the appearance of eventually being a mere monument to men with means.

I remember a missionary couple coming to visit us on one occasion and both remarking quite spontaneously how they wished they could live in a house like ours instead of the large foreign style building provided for them by the Mission Board. They felt that a typical Japanese-style house would bring them so much closer to the people they were trying to reach. They have had their wish. Today, of course, living standards are so high and building styles so altered sometimes it would be difficult to live up to the Japanese 'Joneses'.

A missionary friend, whom we met immediately on his return from furlough in the States, told how he was attending a big conference of Home Board Mission leaders and was staggered at the sums they insisted as necessary for the support of their missionaries. They would not believe he could live and work on the figures he gave them. Another missionary couple has told us frankly that many more missionaries could be sent abroad if the Home Board did not demand such a high promised support before they were permitted to sail.

The missionary society that works on a fixed budget and promised support naturally tends to be critical of the 'irresponsible' society that promises nothing. They may even have heard of the skeleton of a missionary reputed to have been found in African jungles with the badge of a faith

missionary society reposing sedately on its bleache
ribs — horrid indictment of a policy that would permit a
missionary to starve to death! Living members of the same
society (915 of us at the moment) are even callous enough to
chuckle at the story.

Hudson Taylor once wrote, 'We might indeed have had a
guarantee fund if we had wished it, but we felt that it was
unnecessary and would do harm. Money wrongly placed
and money given from wrong motives are both greatly to be
dreaded.' (Hudson Taylor's *Spiritual Secret*. Dr. and Mrs.
Howard Taylor, C.I.M. p. 85.) I wonder what he would have
said at the present day tendency to require the promise of
furlough travel allowances, health insurances, retiring funds
and old age benefits before leaving for overseas, not to mention incidentals like a car fund, adequate housing and very
large sums for the education of the children. It is to be
hoped that missionaries from the Third World will not be
encouraged to think the same way about missions. Whether
material assurances are given or not, we trust there will be
such a heaven-sent constraint of the Spirit upon them that
priorities will be maintained and they will be obedient to the
Heavenly vision.

When faith mission principles were being born out of the
travail of the early days of the C.I.M. we notice that Hudson
Taylor was deeply concerned about the missionary having a
non-monetary motive. In the statement in the book mentioned above, that is expressly dealt with, but there are also
other reasons for the emphasis upon making no appeal for
funds and so I want to quote the whole passage.

The work they were undertaking was far too great to be
limited to any one denomination. He felt it necessary to
seek the co-operation of believers irrespective of denomination, as long as they held to firm belief in the inspiration
of the Scriptures. Then the fact that the Mission would
offer no salaries would help to deter all but those whose
experience made them sure of God. The new enterprise

should not deflect men or means from existing agencies. He hoped to open up a new way for workers who might not be acceptable to other societies, whose preparation had not included a university training. No one would be asked to join the Mission. If the Lord of the Harvest wanted them in the particular field where the Mission was working then He would put it into their hearts to apply. If the Mission could be sustained in answer to prayer, without subscription lists or solicitation of any kind for funds, it might grow up among the older societies without danger of diverting gifts from their accustomed channels.

Obviously he also felt that a work of God that was not dependent upon men and methods could be a singular testimony to the faithfulness of God.

There was no criticism of existing denominational missions and none was implied. However, the need was more likely to be met by believers from different churches and so interdenominational faith missions were born. At one time, one could presume that if it was interdenominational then it was also a mission that made no appeal for funds, but that is not necessarily so today.

Then the fact that no appeals were to be made meant that there would be no competition for the interest and support of Christians in any way. That meant, if the work was to be supported at all, the Lord would have to touch hearts directly without the usual media for touching people's hearts to give. News for prayer, yes. Information designed to awaken the conscience of Christians about their responsibility to take the Gospel abroad, yes, lots of it. But the new missionary depended upon the Lord to equip and sustain. So today, even if there is only sufficient to pay the fare to the country, the society takes this as one sign, I repeat, one sign and not the only sign, that the Lord is thrusting this person forth to serve Him abroad. With some, the money for fares comes in at the eleventh hour, but the young

missionary goes forward confident that the Lord will continue to supply all that is needed.

I am aware that some Christian leaders at home are
known to urge prospective missionaries to seek out a
mission that offers guaranteed support. The argument is that
the Home Board should take every precaution to protect the
new missionary: it should itself exercise the faith to see that
the workers get adequate support and not leave this extra
burden among all the others that the new missionary will
have to shoulder. 'They will have enough to contend with' is
the argument. Norman Grubb rightly asks if faith for daily
needs is a burden and something 'to contend with'?

Then I hear another critic saying, 'That's all very well, but
how do you account for the fact that I know of a missionary
belonging to one of these faith societies who has been
stranded and had to be helped out financially by some other
missionary belonging to one of the denominational boards?
Has faith been more than he could contend with?' In other
words, the missionary not only has less this way, not only
none, but sometimes is a burden on other missionaries who
make no special profession of faith!

The nearest experience we have had of this kind of dilemma arose out of a situation where a missionary got to the
field who should never have left home. It would be quite
wrong to go into the details here but this was a case of
unsuitability which had not been discovered for very special
reasons at the home base. Very soon there was a problem
over finances and eventually a lot of missionaries on the
field were involved financially.

I have heard of one or two other cases but the information is too indirect for me to judge where the breakdown
has taken place. Conceivably it could be through lack of
closely knit teamwork on the part of the home board and its
missionary members either at home or abroad. While the
individual missionary has to have a lively faith he is not
called to exercise it in isolation from others of like faith.
Wesley said that the Bible knows nothing about a solitary

religion. The missionary is very glad to be part of a family of faith, both in the sense of keeping open the lines of communication with home staff and with other members of the team on the field.

Personally, I am profoundly thankful for home staff who, while not committed to finding any stated salary for me on the field, obviously feel a moral and spiritual responsibility keenly and who give themselves to special prayer if there appears to be any lack in general support funds.

Finally, something must be said about the fact that the missionary who looks to the Lord directly for supply may occasionally and momentarily have nothing, and be thankful; he may have less than others and still be very grateful. But there can also be times when he has abundance and naturally be glad of that too. The missionary who is on a fixed salary may not have the same opportunity for surprises! Whether the gift sent for us is $10.00 or $100.00, we get it all. The Lord sends according to our need. Sometimes special gifts come before the need is apparent and so we know a need for its use is coming!

When devaluation took ten per cent off the Canadian dollar and twenty per cent off that of New Zealand, our two respective countries, while others were complaining about the difference it was making in their support figures, we found that ours remained about the same because a few friends were being prompted to raise their gifts to offset the difference and some gifts came from new sources.

I am sure that missionaries with denominational boards and other societies have had the same experience. A missionary can still be looking to the Lord directly no matter whether all his support is sent to him from one congregation at home or is budgeted for in some form of promised support by numbers of faithful friends. It is the heart attitude of the individual missionary that is so important.

Certainly among us all, no matter what method we follow as given of God, there will be total agreement on the need of a spirit of sacrifice. A young Christian teacher whom I know of was challenged to give so much of her income to missions that in a very real sense she had to live by faith. It was a special joy to see the Lord meet her resulting needs in amazing ways. It also proved to be good disciplinary preparation for later missionary service.

It is this type of missionary we need. Lederer and Burdick in their famous book *The Ugly American* write, 'It has been my experience that superior people are attracted only by challenge. By setting our standard low and making our life soft we have automatically and unconsciously assured ourselves of mediocre people.' The missionary should expect to have to make sacrifices and look upon them as part of his credentials as an apostle on the frontiers of the church. To stress security, sufficiently and provision for all foreseeable exigencies is to assure ourselves in some cases at least, of the kind of missionary we don't want.

Epilogue

SELECTING INCIDENTS THAT POINT up some aspects of the life of faith can perhaps over-emphasise the importance of faith itself. Why talk about the 'hand' when the Lord is filling it with the rarest orchids or the most succulent apples? It remains but the hand to receive and certainly does not earn the gifts it gets just by virtue of its man-oeuvrability, or whether or not the fingers are as exquisitely shaped as those of a high-born Japanese maiden.

Many a practising psychologist today will argue that faith itself is of profound healing value. If he is a non-Christian he will insist that faith in anything is better than no faith at all. If the patient is in the West he might be urged to go to church and begin to look away from himself. If he is a Japanese he may expect to find some help in one of the discussion groups regularly conducted by some of the new Buddhist religions that are really up on group therapy.

I recall trying to practise my limited Japanese vocabulary on a farmer resting beside his rice paddy one day after ar-rival in Japan. I understood enough to realise that I was venerated quite highly just by virtue of being a missionary and that faith itself was very important. No matter what faith, as long as you had faith. Some modern Buddhist sects are not so tolerant nor so eclectic. Neither am I, but for a different reason!

Faith itself is a neutral factor. To be of real value it has to be linked with some object that makes it dependable in its exercise. The hand can ignorantly grasp gelignite as well as apples; it is the head that decides one to be dangerous and the other delicious. To change the figure: a missionary I know had faith to believe that her train was going in one direction but through ignorance of the written directions on the carriages she settled blissfully into the seat, only to be whisked off in the opposite direction from where she wanted to go. Her faith was misplaced. The object was unreliable, or rather, her untaught faith led her to trust the wrong thing. Obviously it is one of Satan's occupations to get people to put implicit trust in some man-pleasing alternative to the truth. The more religious it is the better. The more one train looks like another, the more easily the weary commuter will be deceived into boarding the wrong one!

As evangelical Christians I can see some dangers in our emphasising faith alone. It is not uncommon for some to say in response to some challenge, 'Let's believe for so and so . . .' The thought is that just by believing together for something, if we believe hard enough, sincerely enough, and unwaveringly enough, it will come to pass. One of our Lord's own promises in the context of simple faith seems to read just like that. Mark 11:20–24, '. . . whatever you ask in prayer, believe that you receive it, and you will.' Perhaps a balanced exegesis to this passage can be found by pointing out that what the Lord is emphasising here is the need for really believing when we believe, sincere faith rather than emphasising the 'whatever'. In other words, it is not an open sesame to ask for anything we could possibly wish for, but that when we are asking, to really believe we are going to get it, or it is meaningless faith. There are other passages where the Lord is talking about prayer and where He emphasises the conditions for their being answered. One has to do with asking in His Name, which I take to mean that it needs to be something consistent with His Person and work (John 16:24). Another has to do with both abiding in Him and His words abiding in us — thus thoroughly conditioning our very thinking processes so that our asking is consistent with His will for us (John 15:7).

Therefore when we 'take a stand of faith' either for ourselves or for anyone else, it is not the believing itself that is the important thing; it is what we believe and whether or not the thing asked is the will of God or not.

Tim Lahaye in his excellent book, *Transformed Temperaments* (Tyndale House p. 147) very honestly tells of how he and his church were involved in the purchase of expensive property and he says that after much prayer and work, 'our people caught the vision to trust God for the impossible'. Their plan to build a church on this property resulted in litigation with politicians for about two years and they finally turned it down. He had prayed over this place, walked over and claimed it just as others had done for theirs and it had worked for them. Why not for him? When writing the book they still had no solution for their property but the Lord had taken away their depression and discouragement. They came to believe that the Lord has some better place for them.

We know others who have made public claims that something was shortly to come to pass because they 'had trusted for it', but nothing came of it.

I see similar dangers in the emphasis upon faith in the ministry of healing. Some urge that if we had faith enough then all our sickness would be healed. I realise that a whole theology of healing in relation to the atonement is involved, because the thought is that the Lord came not only to cleanse us from sin but also to heal us of our diseases. That some are miraculously healed through faith and God's intervention goes without saying, but I also know only too well that some with the liveliest faith are not healed. Often it is not the imperfection of faith that permits one of the Lord's servants to suffer disability. There are too many other factors to be considered and the criticism of the person's faith can lead to real and unnecessary distress.

God is sovereignly at work in some areas, such as part of

Indonesia, and miracles have taken place that have evoked a storm of controversy. My purpose here is not to discuss the credibility of the alleged miracles, for sufficient have undoubtedly happened to show that the Lord is at work through His people. The thing I want to point out is that very simple folk have often been used in a special way. It could be argued that their very simplicity made them especially useable. Like children they would take the Lord just at His Word and act upon it accordingly. It would follow therefore if we could all return to a childlike simplicity of faith, we should similarly see the Lord at work through us. Perhaps it has been for this reason that efforts were made by Western Christians to get one of the women specially used in a healing ministry to visit the Western churches. Apparently her air-fare was sent for this very purpose, but the sad result was that through this she suddenly felt that she herself had become 'someone' and her faith out of the ordinary. Apparently she drifted away from the Lord and I would lay the blame squarely on the Western Christians in their unthinking zeal for the spectacular.

There are a number of factors in the present revival in Indonesia that are quite unique; it would seem that the Lord suits the methods of His working to the culture, the disposition, and to the times of the people involved. Just to marvel at their faith alone is to ignore a number of factors that have gone to make up the faith they have, and probably at the same time not to appreciate the dangers that specially attend some of the manifestations of God in this way.

Calvin said that we are saved by faith alone, but it is the kind of faith that is never alone. There are the concomitant factors of a true repentance and a real change in disposition. These and others could no doubt all be included in the 'good works' emphasised by James. But what I want to stress in this concluding chapter is not so much the things that accompany faith but the things that generate a biblical faith and make it so important as our side of a wonderful partnership with God.

Paul argues that faith comes from hearing the preaching of Christ (Romans 10:17) or what he also calls in verse 8, 'the word of faith which we preach'. In those days before the writing of the New Testament people were more dependent than now upon the preached or 'gossiped' Gospel. Today we can justifiably say that faith comes by the Word of God and grows in proportion to being gripped by it, and is contagious in proportion to our revelling in it.

Faith grows shaky in proportion to the disuse of the Bible in daily life; it becomes warped in proportion to our abuse of the Bible, using it merely as a commentary or supplementary text for our own experience.

The Bible directs our attention and our worship towards the Lord Jesus Himself. In Hebrews 12:2 He is Himself called the pioneer and perfecter of our faith: we are urged to look to Jesus as such as we run the race set before us. The context for this exhortation suggests that the stimulus for looking to Jesus in this way comes from the cloud of witnesses whose faith is pictured for us so graphically in chapter 11.

In other words, faith begets faith. Faith is contagious. Fear certainly is, so why not its direct opposite? The faith of a George Müller certainly encouraged the faith of a Hudson Taylor and that of many another like him. We are told expressly to imitate the faith of those who have been over us in the Lord (Hebrews 13:7). We can do this without a slavish mimicry of the persons themselves.

The very diversity of faith's expression in the lives of the men and women portrayed in Hebrews 11 has been an encouragement to me. In verse 3 the faith of us all is described as understanding how the world was made. Faith in Abel (verse 4) expressed itself in discerning the kind of offering that would be acceptable to God and he soon found himself the object of his brother's hatred. The Cains have been hating the Abels ever since. Then faith in Enoch (verse 5) meant walking with God for 300 years. The sudden translation into heaven probably did not catch him by surprise!

In verse 7 we have Noah, through faith, acting upon the prophetic warnings of coming judgment; in this sense it is hardly wrong for faith to be fearful. He was to spend the next hundred years or so, no doubt, amidst the most aggravating mockery, grotesque caricatures, cartoons, and lampoons, building the biggest demonstrated sermon of all time. If it is true, as some suggest, that there had been no rainfall till the flood came and that plant growth had thrived on the heavy dews, it would point up the peerless patience of Noah's faith even more, and its total belief in the naked word of God. He would not even be able to imagine how God was going to fulfil His warnings and this would add a sharp barb to the invective of the mocking crowd.

With verse 8 we are introduced to Abraham the father of the faithful, and with him we have faith obeying (verse 8), sojourning (verse 9) and sacrificing (verse 17). The two major crises of his leaving his birthplace and then late in life offering up Isaac, were characterised by instant obedience. It was the sojourning periods that constituted the biggest test of his faith. It was during this period he gave way to lies to protect his own skin, and then gave way to Sarah's insistence that he produce an heir by Hagar, and thus try to help the Lord fulfil His own promises. The unexciting humdrum day-by-dayness of the patience of faith can test faith at its inner core. But it is still Abraham who gets the accolade for faith and is used in Paul's classic passage in Romans to describe the faith that is 'constantly anticipating the birth of those things that give as yet no token of their existence' (Romans 4:17, translation by Way). The Lord seemed deliberately to wait till there was no possibility of children by natural birth before fulfilling His promise towards Abraham and his innumerable family to be. There is a fullness of time for the things that the Lord does. It would appear that He waits till we are shut up to faith alone, and can't think of a single further suggestion to make!

When we come to Moses (Hebrews 11:24–25) choosing to share ill treatment with the people of God (verse 26) it would indicate that he had faith in the future of his own people when no future could have been dimmer and when he himself felt he was the last one to help them. How it comes through again and again in the record of the faithful that they themselves are surprised at the way the Lord promises them the impossible, calls for the inconceivable and does the totally unexpected!

Perhaps the writer had this in mind when he mentions in verse 33 that some 'received promises'. That does not sound very exciting alongside — no — in between subduing kingdoms on the one hand, and stopping the mouth of lions on the other! Perhaps there is a cause and effect relationship. I wonder what promise Daniel received as he slipped down among the kings of beasts?

Faith, therefore, is not divorced from understanding, discerning, walking, fearing, obeying, sojourning, sacrificing, choosing and receiving. But perhaps faith reaches its peak in its 'love relationship'. Paul says in Galatians 5:6 that faith works by love. In 1 Corinthians 13 he says, 'though I have faith to remove mountains and have not love I am nothing'. We know that we love the Lord Jesus because He first loved us and gave Himself for us. We trust Him because we love Him. I am sure that that is the order that He prefers, because if there is any sacrifice in the life of faith, then it should be just because 'sacrifice is the ecstasy of giving the best we have to the One we love the most'.

I find it necessary and helpful on occasion to ask myself some personal questions.

'Am I just following a safe pattern of faith in daily life because I inherited it from others and am accustomed to it? Do I live like this just because it is the done thing in my circle and I don't want to get out of step?'

'With age do I find myself with an accommodating faith? Has the keen cutting edge of early moral distinctiveness given way to softness of life and tolerance of known evil?'

'Do I really have faith in the life-changing power of the

Word of God today — minus my astute explanations and exposition, that is?'

'Do I really believe the Lord is guiding my beloved brother (sister) just as definitely as He has done me, even if he does walk such an odd path? What does he think about *my* guidance?'

'Is there something totally disarming and unsophisticated about my faith before others? Is it real? Is it professional? Am I a bit of a showman? Do I have to have an audience to practise faith?'

'Can I take the shocks of calamity and share the griefs of those around me today any more redemptively than I could in the first glow of new-found faith?'

'How often have I lifted my heart in the discipline of praise this week? Has the sameness of the walk of faith over the last few years dulled the sense of privilege?'

'Can I lift my heart to Him today and say, "Lord, I love you and trust you. I refuse to be offended by whatever you permit in my life this day. I know that you chasten me out of love. I know that you wean me from silly, passing things just out of love. I know you want me to love You for what You are, and not for the many things You give to those who trust You." '